World View from Elenora Giddings Ivory Tower

The Life and Times of a Religious Advocate

Nancy,
Keep the faith

Elenora
Sisterhood

Elenora Giddings Ivory

ISBN 978-1-64258-695-4 (paperback)
ISBN 978-1-64258-696-1 (digital)

Christian Faith Publishing, Inc.
832 Park Avenue
Meadville, PA 16335
www.christianfaithpublishing.com

Printed in the United States of America

Contents

Part 6

Part 7

Part 8

Part 9

Part 10

Introduction

A Retrospective

World View from Elenora Giddings Ivory Tower
"Your neck is like an ivory tower.
Your eyes are pools in Heshbon,
by the gate of Bath-rabbim."
—Song of Solomon 7:4

Dear Andrew and Simon,

This collection of essays represents commentary on various events throughout your Nana's life. They are a retrospective view on particular happenings with observations to applicable current events. I hope they will not only interest you, but inform you as well.

A professor once told my Douglass College Political Science 101 class that the movement of historic events is like a swinging pendulum that sways back and forth, but never really goes back to as far as it began. Another way of saying, two steps forward and one step back, if we are learning from history.

I use the term "Ivory Tower" here while knowing that it is an unflattering description, because throughout my working life as an advocate for issues of justice, that is what I was sometimes accused of—accused of being in an idealistic impermeable "Ivory Tower" when it came to the issues of the day.

According to Wikipedia, *"The term **ivory tower** originates in the Biblical Song of Solomon (7:4). The term has been used to designate an environment of intellectual pursuit disconnected from the practical concerns of everyday life. In American English usage, it is also used as shorthand for academia or the university."*

I contend that the issues and events in these essays—the actions of my life—are not *"disconnected from practical concerns of everyday life."* They reflect the plight in which many parts of humanity find themselves, whenever human rights and human dignity are denied to some of us.

Particularly, my time in the Washington office right after the reunion of the former Northern and Southern streams of the Presbyterian Church were often referred to as a lightning rod, meaning that often the office and me in particular took the negative strikes from those in the church who did not want to see some of the General Assembly approved polices used in our writings or in advocacy in Washington. We were frequently written about in the *Layman*—a Para-church publication that saw itself as a watchdog concerning issues that might be too liberal in their mind. Some of these issues are below.

These years of ministry often felt like being in the "Belly of the Whale" along with biblical Jonah who tried to avoid his calling to ministry, but ultimately, he went forward. As you read this, and I hope you do, know that the Apostle Paul tells us in Romans that we do not need to always be resistant to government. Because our citizenry is made up of different cultures with differing mores, as a way of bringing some semblance of societal civility we can obey and follow the "Civil Magistrate as long as the Civil Magistrate" (Romans 13:1–7) is following God on behalf of us all.

I hope and pray that anyone reading this will come to understand that those of us in the northern parts of these United States have also experienced incidents of intense racism. It was not just in the southern states. Racial aggression is not only physical, but it is also emotional and verbal. Impactful white supremacy will show itself in several of the essays included here.

For openers, I remember that when I was hired to work as a cashier in the local A&P and then later at the ShopRite Supermarket, some of my older first cousins thought I had landed a white person's job. Black folks did not get those level jobs in those days (1965–1973). The white store manager, who did not hire me, could not quite figure me out and always looked at me as though I were an anomaly. He certainly did not understand that sometimes I was going off to participate or lead in national Presbyterian events, after all from his perspective who would want to hear anything that I had to say. He was never harassing, just puzzled. Looking back, he may never have traveled very far, and I did for church events.

In 1988, the late Rev. Robert Curry, formerly from a northern Virginia church, sent a three-page complementary critique of one of my sermons. His words kind of sums up my seventy-plus years of life. He said, *"You are a black female ordained preacher. That is three minorities! God, you must have had to fight ten thousand times ten thousand demons. Tell us about them. Let us know how the battle goes. Tell us about those demons "out there" (for there we sit!) And tell us about those demons "inside you" that no one, no one, but you, uniquely you can tell us about. Witness for us!"*

Part 1

Part I

1953: First Brush with Political Advocacy: Manalapan and Water for Housing

Presidency of Harry S. Truman and Dwight David Eisenhower

"I was thirsty and you gave me something to drink."
—Matthew 35:25

My first awareness of a time of church activism happened when I was a very young member of Westminster Presbyterian Church of Manalapan, New Jersey. We referred to it simply as Manalapan Church. It was located off Highway 33 on Conover Road just outside of Freehold, New Jersey.

Across the street from Manalapan Church was migrant labor housing. It was one of the places where some African American families lived year round. In 1953, my family moved there from Philadelphia where I was born. I was about eight years old. The family was my father Edward Littleton Giddings Sr. (1903–1958) and my mother Phoebe Hill Giddings (1915–1987), along with my younger brothers, Edward Jr., Nathaniel, and Tyrone. Younger sisters Phoebe Janet and Ella had not yet been born.

We lived there for just one year, while my father builds from the ground up himself a three-bedroom, one-bath house in nearby Clarksburg. We were happy to move into our new house with its unfinished interior walls, even though it was only completed on the outside as a way to stave off the pending winter of 1954.

Unlike the Manalapan migrant house, our new house had an indoor toilet and not an outhouse. (A picture of me standing in front of one of the track houses is below.) Our new house had running water from a sink and not a farm-type pump in the kitchen of this two-room cabin. And there was a real bathtub instead of a metal tub.

When we lived at Manalapan, this was the time I became involved with the Manalapan Church. My father would gather us all up, his children and some nieces, nephews and neighbors, and drive us the little ways across and down the road to the Church on Easter Sunday. He must have thought it was a long service Baptist Church, because we had to wait outside for him to pick us up for what seemed like a long, long time after the service. I cannot remember if it was Rev. Echelberger or Rev. James Aaron Mitcham Jr. who waited patiently with us.

Manalapan Church allowed me to feel that I was worthy of being a human being. My Millstone Township Elementary School classes where not segregated in the way you would see in the south. But the black and white students played together in an impersonal way. This was not unfriendly, but not close and buddy-buddy either. I had the feeling of just being there. This was a small community. The Rev. Patricia Budd Kepler, one of the very early women to be ordained in the Presbyterian Church, became the pastor during my teenage years. It was she who challenged me to apply to Harvard Divinity School. I am most grateful for this and am eternally thankful.

This Church was a Revolutionary War–era structure that was built on large tree basis. As is often the case, the small African American congregation could not afford the upkeep that was probably maintained when the congregation was more grand, wealthy, and white.

The state highway department approached the Presbytery of Monmouth, where the church was owned, with an offer to buy it as the State wanted to build one of the now infamous turnoff-jug handles as Highway 33 was being widened. We were politically and financially powerless in our efforts to stop the sale and be allowed to keep worshipping as a congregation.

The state also tore down the migrant labor housing when the residents ask to get running water installed in the military barrack style housing. The answer was no. We thought, that is what happens sometimes, when you ask for water.

With the church and the housing gone, the families of the congregation were scattered. It was probably seen, by the authorities, to be easier to tear down the housing than it would have been to put running water into them.

I sympathize with the people of Flint, Michigan. The people of Flint, Michigan, are still asking for clean water years after their supply had been found to be contaminated with lead. In 2017, weeks after Hurricane Maria devastated Puerto Rico, the people were still in need of clean water. We have to ask if this delay is due to the fact that they are people of color. The cry goes out that we are all Americans, yet some of us have to beg for clean, life-sustaining water.

Our family had already moved out of the Manalapan housing years before it reached that point of demolition. As bad as it was, it was seen as the best of the housing camps where many of the African Americans lived. Pergola Ville, another camp not too far away, had dirt floors within cabins that looked like the old time slave cabins. This was the 1960s!

During my early elementary school day, the interior walls of our home were eventually covered in sheet rock as my father, Edward Littleton Giddings Sr. (1903–1958), labored to put on the finishing touches. He was a skilled construction worker, who did the roofing, plumbing, carpentry, electrical, and almost anything that needed to be done on our home as well as his sister's and nieces' homes that were being built next door. By day, he worked in the growing construction industry. It was the need for labor that brought the family to New Jersey from Philadelphia when I was eight years old.

Edward Littleton Giddings Sr. would often be asked to step in when someone else was not able to finish out a task on a construction job. He gladly stepped in. On March 29, 1958, he climbed down into a newly dug foundation ditch to figure something out as the construction company built the Kendall Park Division. They did not stop the moving bulldozer equipment above and the ditch caved in on him, and he was gone instantly.

That day, I saw three cars travel down the driveway to give my mother this unbelievable news. I was twelve years old at this time. Your uncles were ten, eight, and six years old. Your aunts were two and one. His trait of stepping in when someone else cannot seem to complete a task seems to have been handed down to me and my siblings. He described himself as a jack of all trades and master of none and that he worked from "kin to can't"—meaning, that you worked from the time you can see by the sun until you can't see by it in the evening. Therefore, in justice ministry, we advocate for safe labor laws. Had the ditch been fortified with barriers along its sides, your grandfather might have lived a longer life.

What I remember most about him is that he was so proud of the fact that the older of his children could all read. He was denied an education in his segregated Cape Charles, Virginia school system and only completed the third grade. He made a mark. He did not write a signature. He was so proud that his children could read that he once handed me the New Jersey driver's manual and asked me to read a little of it to him and his friends to brag that I could read. He and his friends had to study the illustrative parts of the manual.

In the fifties, sixties, and seventies we fought for integrated schools as way to bring education to our community so that we had fewer of those who could not read. We now focus on quality education, because integration, if it happened, did not always bring with it a quality education. We also wanted to be treated fairly.

When a local news report told a story of a young white girl who scored very high on an IQ test aired on TV, the next day my teacher entered the classroom and asked if we had all seen that story. He said it was a big deal, but that someone in his class scored just as high, but he could not say who. Then he glanced at me, and as he turned his head, he muttered, "What a waste." That was how I learned that I was "intelligent." So incidents like this were part of my early formative years.

August 1971: The Ku Klux Klan "Visit" and Historic Monuments

Presidency of Richard M. Nixon

> *He said to him, "'you shall love the Lord your God with all your heart, and with all your soul, and with all your mind.' This is the greatest and first commandment. And a second is like it: 'You shall love your neighbor as yourself.' On these two commandments hang all the law and the prophets."*
> —Matthew 22:37–40

Sometimes I just want to ask people what is it about these two commandments from Jesus that you do not understand, especially if you profess to be a Christian, or even more broadly, a person of faith in the God of us all?

I type this as I watch the events of the Charlottesville, VA, unfold on this August 12, 2017, day. There is violence erupting over the possible removal of a statute in commemoration of Confederate General Robert E. Lee in a public park. Groups representing the Ku Klux Klan (KKK), Alt-Right, Nazi sympathizers, and others are there to protest this removal. To some of them, it simply marks a historic event and has nothing to do with racism. They fail to accept that the historic event the statue represents is one where racist views of enslavement were being protected.

As I watch these events, I am reminded of the time when the Federal Bureau of Investigation (FBI) came knocking at our door in the middle of the day. At the time, your grandfather Tommie Ivory

Sr., your mother Cynthia, and your Uncle "T" (Tom) and I lived on Fort Plains Road, in Howell Township, NJ.

I was alone at home and in the kitchen at the sink while cutting up a chicken for dinner when I heard the knock. Since I was in a hurry, I invited him back to the kitchen so that I could continue to prepare the chicken. I now wonder if it was unwise of me to be handling a knife in front of an FBI agent, but I proceeded as he asked questions about the tension in the rural community where we lived.

This FBI "visit" was prompted by recent activity against the African American Community from the local KKK. The Howell Township Booster used my August 1971 letter to the press as the primary basis of their story.

The FBI agent tried to explain the hateful actions against us as within the rights of United States Constitutional First Amendment free speech. He said that we may not always like what we hear, but everyone has the right of free speech—even the Klan. President Donald Trump's remarks about the Charlottesville protestors, equating them all with having wrong intentions, reminded me of this FBI agent's comments—"*There is wrong on both sides.*"

In those Howell Township events, tensions were raised as black mothers approached the school board to ask that the system include books with multiracial pictures and varied cultural understanding for *all* the students. This tension came about because one of our African American children had been sent home with an assignment to write about their family's heritage.

The child's grandmother wrote on the assignment that she was not taught about her African American history in school, and there were no books at her grandchild's school to teach him and therefore he should be excused from the assignment. How could he write about his heritage if it had not been taught to either his parents or his grandparents? Our families wanted to know more about ourselves. We wanted to say more than that we were from slavery. To only speak of slavery leaves only that image in the minds of all of us. Our achievements and triumphs also need to be known and taught.

Our approach to the school board sparked the hate group to come forward and say that no such changes should be made to the way history is taught. According to the Howell Booster, *"Some residents claimed the board was going to 'put in black studies and get rid of reading, writing and arithmetic."*[1]

An August 18, 1971, letter to the Editor of the Howell Booster purported to have been signed by the Exalted Cyclops of the Howell Township Chapter of the United Klan's of America Inc. and also signed by a Mr. Williams—it went so far as to say,

> *"We would like to make it known that we as Klansmen and Klanswomen are not going to tolerate the black action group's activities in Howell Township or any other surrounding towns or counties. We as a large body of Klansmen are going to do everything in our power to stop the group's action against our schools.*
>
> *"Our organization is dedicated to the purpose of never permitting this take-over by the blacks of our community occurring at any time now or in the future."* The letter stated that the KKK thought that Howell was, *"a wonderful place to live . . . move to another area which would suit their purposes better."*

The request to write about our heritage was given during the springtime ending days of the school year. The tensions simmered through the summer. There were cross burnings, KKK leaflets[2] strewn in some neighborhoods and the contents of emptied garbage cans spread on the lawns of some of us. The local authorities reported that they saw no such disruption with trash as we had already cleaned up our properties.

On August 21, 1971, the Booster reported that the person who burned the cross on public land was identified and charged. They never published his name for fear of further violence against him, his family, or his home. The paper stated that, *"The man was released on $1,000 bail after being arraigned before Municipal Court Judge John W. Cavanagh on a charge of "Maliciously burning a cross."* His crudely constructed burning cross was thrown across Manassa and Old Tavern Road. He was a local white man and a member of the KKK.

In the wake of all this, we formed a support group called *Citizens for Progressive Action of Howell Township (CPA)*. We were a small group of mothers and a few men.

On August 23, 1971, CPA was slated to appear before the Board of Education to advance our request. Mr. William L. Wardell, president of the Howell Township Board of Education, said *"The August 23 meeting is a work session to listen to proposals by the CPA. It is not a public meeting."* He also let it be known that any other group could also make an appointment with the Board to present their request.

I do not remember that there was any protest against us at that meeting. There were no visible KKK protestors, and we were able to present our case. In fact, these forty-six years later, I do not really remember much from the actual meeting. But from the September 16, 1971, Booster article, my memory was jogged with this quote from board President Wardell,

> *"On Monday, August 23, the Board met in executive session with the CPA at the Land O'Pines School. There were two items on the agenda for discussion, the educational curriculum and the school calendar for the 1971-72 academic year.*
>
> *"As a result of this meeting, an understanding was reached that the superintendent of schools, with his professional staff, will continue revisions of the curriculum and studying and developing a multi-ethnic curriculum. It was also agreed between the CPA and the board that the Martin Luther King, Day, Jan 15 would again be included on the list of days of in-school observances as was done last year."*

It was not that we were asking for something that did not exist in other jurisdictions. Multiracial-multiethnic educational materials were available for usage in order to show that "Dick and Jane," etc., did not have to be portrayed as white only.

Our additional request was that Martin Luther King's birthday becomes a holiday in the school system. We were told that the academic calendar was already prepared for the coming year, but that the faculty would plan appropriate assemblies for the occasion.

Twelve years later, on November 2, 1983, then-president Ronald Reagan signed the bill as proposed by Representative Katie Hall of Indiana that created a federal holiday honoring Dr. King. This bill passed the House of Representatives by a count of 338 to 90. This was a veto-proof margin. Dr. Martin Luther King Jr. Day became a federal holiday and was observed for the first time on January 20, 1986.

The presidential signing was twelve years after our request to the Howell Township Board of Education. By this time, your mother, Uncle T, and I were living in Albany, New York. This Howell Township event was my second brush with political advocacy.

With each victory come setbacks through the efforts of those who want to snatch it away. Or there comes a redaction of the original understanding. Although MLK Jr. Day was eventually handled as an in service day in many schools before it became a federal holiday where the schools would actually be closed and people would have a day free from work, there were those who tried to rename the day to "Brotherhood Day." That was the experience my niece Benita had as she was in her elementary school class.

Once the holiday was a reality, her teacher announced that they would be observing "Brotherhood Day." Benita, in the sixth grade of her Brownsville, New Jersey School, said to the teacher that it was Martin Luther King Jr. Day. She would not back down from this ascertain and my sister Ella had to go to the school to say that her child should not be corrected; it is Dr. Martin Luther King Jr. Day.

Goings-on, as simple as driving from place to place, were not always easy either. Even though we were in a rural small community and an hour away from both Philadelphia and New York City, I remember being stopped by local and state police many times during those days of civil unrest in the larger cities. I did not understand why this happening until a friend pointed out that I fit the general description of Angela Davis, as well as Joanne Deborah Chesimard who was being sought by authorities through an FBI wanted poster with a million-dollar reward for her capture being offered. Chesimard was called a domestic terrorist on the poster. She had been active with something called the *Black Liberation Army*. At the time, she was considered armed and dangerous and was in the New Jersey area. She now goes by the name of Assata Shakur and has been in exile in Cuba.

Elenora Ivory

My children remember one such stop when they were in the back seat of our car. As I was pulled over in our white 1967 Chevy Impala, I instructed them to stay quiet, keep their hands in their laps as I kept mine on the steering wheel, and to not move around.

Cynthia remembers the officer being mean with an attitude that did not seem necessary at the time. She was probably about eight or nine years old. He finally told us to move on along. There was no explanation about why we were stopped.

As we go back to where I started with this article, at the Charlottesville protest and the removal of symbols that, I believe, represent a time of insurrection and violence, I could never understand why the nation has allowed the veneration of those who once tried to overthrow the US government. Under other circumstances, this would be called terrorism. Or perhaps even treason. *Webster's Dictionary* describes treason as, *"the offense of attempting by overt acts to overthrow the government of the state to which the offender owes allegiance or to kill or personally injure the sovereign or the sovereign's family."*

Furthermore, the insurrectionist did not want to "love their neighbor as they loved themselves." All of humanities' creative and inventive potentials in people should be allowed to flourish. What has this world lost by denying the livelihood of some of its citizens?

But I have come to pity the racist. Pity may be a more powerful strike against them then hate. No one wants to be pitied. I believe that there is a part of pity that presents a factor that the pitied one has not yet attained a much sought-after desired goal. And that desired goal here is to not be open to all that each of us has to offer.

What if one of the men they hung during the Jim Crow years could have brought about a cure for some affliction we still face in society, if only he could have been given a chance to do so? We will never know because hatred was allowed to be engaged. They do not know what they are denying in their lives. Pity is a stronger emotion than hatred. Pity indicates that I find you wanting of something. Maybe a response to racist and racism is to throw them one big "pity party."

I began this essay by discussing the current controversy over public monuments. I firmly believe that monuments to those who tried to undo the nation are not in the best interest of a nation that is still trying to present a united front for its entire people. Should there be monuments to Germany's Adolf Hitler or the Soviet Union's Joseph Stalin? Of course not.

Why cannot segments of our population understand that these Confederate monuments would not be in the best interest of a desired empathetic public? Put these monuments in museums. Confederate monuments venerate a time when not all Americans were seen as being entitled to all that this nation has promised to its people.

If we are to have monuments as a way to tell the history of this country and what it stands for, there can be monuments to those who fought for this nation and the affirming ideals it purports to have. I was pleased, some years ago, to find the Centennial Park Ft. Meyers, Florida, monument. It is a military monument which honors the Second Regiment Infantry, US Colored Troops who defended the Federal Post against the Confederate Army at the Battle of Fort Myers (February 20, 1865, during the Civil War).

The Ft. Meyers website goes on to say that

> *The bronze figure "Clayton" represents 1,000 men freed from slavery who enlisted in the Union Army to fight against the attacking Confederate Calvary. The wall with its gate emphasizes the theme of the gateway to freedom from slavery.*
>
> *Ft. Meyers, Florida belonged to the Confederates, but the 2nd Regiment used the fort in this Gulf of Mexico backwater as a base for stealing local cattle—4,000 head in all—which would have supplied Confederate troops in Georgia. In February 1865, Confederates began firing on the Fort. The 2nd Regiment soldiers there held off the attack and causalities were light on both sides.*

This regiment traveled from Virginia to the Florida area and picked up runaway enslaved men along the way who joined them. This story about the Battle of Fort Meyers is a personal one for our family because Private Levin Goffigan Giddings (1845–1928) was part of this regiment. Levin was your great-great-great-grandfather. His military records are at the National Archives in Washington. His name appears on the Monument to Colored Troops in the Shaw District of Washington, DC. His name is badly misspelled as "Lening Gaffigan."

It is not just Levin who fought in the wars of this nation. We have had some member of the family serve in each of the wars going back to the Civil War. Your three maternal uncles served in Vietnam in three different branches of the service and were deployed there at the same time.

Your Uncle Edward Littleton Giddings Jr. served in the Air Force as a communications specialist. Your Uncle National Randolph Giddings (1948–2001) served in the Marines as a ground combat solider and returned suffering the effects of both Agent Orange and posttraumatic stress disorder (PTSD). Your Uncle Tyrone Howard Giddings (1951–2016) served as a conscientious objecting medic in the Army and also returned with PTSD.

This story about military service is not unusual to our family. Many African American families had young men enter the service as a way to escape poverty. There were no academic deferments for many African Americans and other minority groups. If any family has a right to demonstrate or protest some government action, it would be families such as ours.

Part 2

1974–1978:[3] Gloucester Memorial Presbyterian Church (formerly New Life Presbyterian): Stated Supply "The Soiling of Old Glory"

Presidency of Gerald R. Ford and Jimmy Carter

"There is no longer Jew or Greek, there is no longer slave or free, there is no longer male and female; for all of you are one in Christ Jesus."
—Galatians 3:28

These were the tumultuous times in the Boston area as racial violence was part of the daily life of many of those who did not want to integrate the regional school systems. Public recreational areas did not display signs for black and white usage only, but it was generally known where you were or were not welcome in the city—if you were black.

In particular, black folks were not welcome in South Boston, an area of several generations of settled immigrants from European countries—particularly Irish immigrants. It was jokingly stated that there were more Irish in the Boston area than there were in Ireland. Boston did not erupt with racial violence in the sixties as did so many cities across the nation, but it came later.

The Massachusetts Legislature enacted the 1965 Racial Imbalance Act, which ordered the state's public schools to desegregate. To achieve this, the Massachusetts Court system ordered desegregation of public schools between 1974 and 1988 through a system of busing students. Judge W. Arthur Garrity Jr. of the United

States District Court for the District of Massachusetts laid out a plan for compulsory busing of students between predominantly white and black areas of the city. It brought racial protests and civil unrest that garnered national attention.

We were in the Boston area because after getting my bachelor's degree from New Jersey's Douglass College of Rutgers University in political science and history in the spring of 1973, your mother Cynthia and your Uncle "T" and I moved to Arlington, MA, which is just outside of Cambridge where I would be attending Harvard Divinity School as I worked toward my three year master of divinity degree and then later being ordained by the former United Presbyterian Church in September 1976.

These were the days of racial tensions in the greater Boston area. I no longer had that white Chevy Impala, but now drove a car that had trouble with its gas indicator sticking at the halfway mark. I forgot to fill it and was out of gas in the driveway of our rented duplex on 18 Walnut Court. I walked to the next block to get a can full of gas to get me to the station to fill it up. The gas station owner filled up the can and walked back with me to my car to fill it up. He did not want me to be walking alone with that can in my hand. There had been a recent story from another part of the country where someone took a can of gas and poured it over a black woman and set her on fire. He did not know me, but he did not want that to happen to me. This is an indication of how much tensions were strained in many parts of the country.

In another incident, I needed to get to the bank, but the Arlington Branch of my bank was closed. Hard to imagine, but I do not remember ATM machines existing at that time. So I drove to nearby Belmont, MA, a town just next door where there would be an open branch of my bank. I walked in and did my banking quickly and walked back to my car. I was only a few blocks away from the bank when the policeman pulled me over. He said the bank I was just in was being robbed at the time I was there and that I fit the general description of someone who was there. I said, *"You mean there was another black woman in the bank with a large afro?"* He saw my book bag on the seat. He blushed and let me go. So I was stopped on suspicion of bank robbery. How often are black people continually being pulled over for something thought to be suspicious?

Despite all that was happening, the three of us continued with our schooling. Because I came to Harvard Divinity School with student loans from my undergraduate school at Douglass as well as with two children, they offered me full scholarship for the three years and enough cash that got me nearly through the year.

At the end of my second year, the money ran out to soon. The Presbyterian General Assembly Financial Aid Office sent a letter saying that there were others who needed additional scholarship more than I and they would not be sending any. But I am forever grateful to Elder Margarita Winthrop, the widow of one of the former pastors of New Life Presbyterian Church where I would later be ordained as she simply mailed me a personal check for $1,000. It was the supplement that got us through to graduation. I was so sorry to not have known about her funeral service.

Upon completion of my studies and achieving my ordination, I became the supply pastor of what was then known as the New Life Presbyterian Church of Roxbury, MA. It later changed its name to the John Gloucester Memorial Presbyterian Church in honor of the first African American to have become a minister in the Presbyterian Church. This was a predominately African American section of Boston. It was only one of two predominately African American Presbyterian Churches in the Boston Presbytery with its total of twenty-two churches.

At first, I did not know that I was the beginning of a wave of black women to be ordained in the Presbyterian Church and became the third African American woman to achieve this honor.

In much the same way, this was a repeat of my experience with the Manalapan Presbyterian Church in that Gloucester Memorial was a small African American congregation trying to find its greater purpose beyond itself.

In addition to the regular worship services, celebration of communion, baptisms, and caring for one another, they also had a Saturday morning tutoring project for neighborhood children and a ten-week summer vacation Bible school with a lunch feeding program and playground activities for eighty to one hundred children five days a week. The city delivered hot lunches to the church for that many children each and every weekday at no cost to the church because we were in a high poverty area.

These programs continued at the church even in the midst of high racial turmoil in the streets a little distance from the church. The children who came were primarily black, but also white and Hispanic. They would come into the Blue House (social hall) and sit at tables in a racially segregated way. After blessing the food, they were told they had to mix up the tables and sit with someone they did not know before we would serve them. Although they were very young, your mother Cynthia and Uncle "T" helped serve.

Not everyone in the Presbytery understood this to be ministry. What did feeding those children have to do with preaching on Sunday morning, bringing souls to Christ or increasing the church roles—they wanted to know. I was often explaining the theology behind this in real-time of feeding the "*hungry, clothing the naked and welcoming the stranger.*" This project was funded with money from Boston Presbytery, the Synod of the Northeast, and the National Missions Agency of the National Presbyterian Church Offices then in New York. That was when the church had more funds at all levels. The congregation provided the Manse with utilities for us to live in. Now that I was out of divinity school, the various levels of the church provided a combined $7,000 a year annually as the salary.

Of course, this meant that I spent a lot of time explaining and promoting the ministry at Gloucester in order to keep the money coming in. Sometimes that meant flying to various meetings of the Synod as they might have been held anywhere across the eleven states of the Synod of the Northeast.

Life continued to be full of anxious moments; I once got off a plane in a late-evening arrival and mistakenly drove into South Boston. Once I realized my mistaken exit from the airport, I was apprehensive and drove out in such a way that would not have called attention to me as black women in that South Boston neighborhood. I was so happy that it was a dark night.

Weeks earlier, I had already experienced a white man putting his hands on the hood of my car as I was stopped at a busy intersection on Tremont Street as he ferociously declared that I had no right to wear the clergy collar I had on. I did not ask if he was so angry because I was a woman dressed like a priest or that I was black wearing the religious symbol. I think he yelled something like "Who in the hell do you think you are, Martin Luther King?" He obviously did not like Dr. King.

Boston area racial vehemence was shown through an image pictured in the *Boston Herald* American newspaper on April 5, 1976. The picture was entitled *"The Soiling of Old Glory."* The photographer, Stanley Forman, was awarded a Pulitzer Prize for this effort.

The picture shows a white teenager, Joseph Rakes. He is assaulting Ted Landsmark with an American flag draped pole. Mr Landsmark is a black man, a lawyer, and a civil rights activist. This was a protest demonstration against integrating the school system and Joseph Rakes was expressing his right as a citizen against integration.

(From Wikipedia, the free encyclopedia)

The Soiling of Old Glory by Stanley Forman.

This turned out to be an accidental confrontation. Mr. Landsmark later said that he was going to a meeting and had just parked his car. When he came around the corner, he was confronted by the flag being thrust at him. He was knocked to the ground and his glasses where broken, but he was not actually hit with the flag. Mr. Rakes received a two-year suspended jail sentence.

The American flag continues to be at the forefront of racial protest. I regret that the current kneeling at sports events by Colin Kaepernick has been misconstrued by some as a way to disrespect the nation and the troops. It is just the opposite. Those kneeling want to draw attention to the fact that the flag must stand for the freedom of speech, life, liberty, and the pursuit of happiness for all persons.

We want peace. Peacemaking is the ultimate aim. But to quote Pope Paul VI, *"If you want peace, work for justice."* If anyone has the right to get on bended knee at a sports event to protest at the flag that we have not all been given fair treatment or clasped arms to bring recognition to the fact that the flag has not represented all the people all of the time, it is mine. My three brothers and one uncle and great-great-grandfather fought in wars. But my family is not unique.

Part 3

1978–1985: New York State Council of Churches, Albany Advocacy Office Director

Presidency of Jimmy Carter and Ronald Reagan

"In Christ there is no east or West-In Him no South or North, But one great fellowship of love through-out the whole wide earth."[4]

60 Minutes CBS Attack on the National Council of Churches of Christ USA

When I entered my office at 362 State Street, where the New York State Council of Churches advocacy office was located, the phone was ringing constantly with angry people who heard our telephone number repeated over and over again on the radio. In response to a conservative radio host going on and on about how awful the Geneva-based World Council of Churches (WCC) was for its *Programme to Combat Racism* and how the WCC was using hard earned contributions from US individuals and member churches as a way to support radical insurgencies in various parts of the world, this talk show host urged all who were listening to call their ecumenical councils to complain and to ask for their money back. No regular work could be done for days until the director of the New York State Council of Churches, the Rev. Dr. Jon Reiger, threatened to sue him. The radio host was not giving correct information about the networking of Councils of Churches locally, regionally, nationally, or internationally.

Each council, at whatever level, is separately incorporated and structured. What this talk show host did not understand was that each council had its own agenda and program focus. Their account-ability is to the member denominations at each council level. Each council has its own structure and responsibilities. As followers of Christ, every denominational church body is often represented at each level of our ecumenical work together.

It, therefore, seemed almost surreal to me and everyone else who was connected to the national church structures that we would be undergoing this distorted attack. As we watched the 7:00 p.m. *60 Minutes* program in January of 1983 unfold on our home screens, we could hardly believe the misinformation and lack of knowledge being presented to the public about the work of the World Council of Churches. The *Readers Digest* and *Time Magazine* also carried similar stories regarding this project.

> *The creation of the Programme to Combat Racism (PCR) was a turning point in the World Council of Churches' (WCC) longstanding opposition to racism. Since its inception, the PCR has been one of the most controversial of the WCC's initiatives. The initial five-year programme concentrated on white racism in South Africa. With the end of apartheid in South Africa, the PCR shifted its attention to the struggle of indigenous peoples and the problem of land rights, as well as to the plight of racially and ethnically oppressed minorities around the world.*[5]

As the *Programme to Combat Racism* supported the work of those on the ground who were fighting against various manifestations of oppression, they were accused by detractors who were claiming that these violent groups were being supported by church and other nonprofit organizations. Or if a group was engaging in actions against oppression, that action might have been labeled negatively.

You can find these words on Wikipedia that clearly are written by someone who did not agree with the idea of the PCR—

The Programme to Combat Racism was a political programme of the World Council of Churches during the 1970s, 1980s and 1990s. It funded a number of liberation movements while those groups were involved in violent struggle, including UNITA and the MPLA in Angola; FRELIMO in Mozambique; SWAPO in South West Africa/Namibia; the Patriotic Front in Rhodesia/Zimbabwe; and the ANC and Pan Africanist Congress in South Africa. According to Rachel Tingle, between 1979 and 1991 the PCR gave a total of $9,749,500 to such groups. "In 1970, Reader's Digest suggested that the PCR was contributing to fourteen groups involved in revolutionary guerrilla activities, some of which were Communist in ideology and receiving arms from the Soviet Union.

To dissuade others from joining them, anytime an oppressed group agitated to undo racism, they were and are often still accused of being political. As we watched the 7:00 p.m. *60 Minutes* program in January of 1983 unfold on our home screens, we could hardly believe the misinformation and lack of knowledge being presented to the public, about the work of the World Council of Churches.

The National Council of Churches, with its headquarters at 475 Riverside Drive in New York City, also issued a seven-page statement:

The January 23 edition of "60 Minutes" (CBS), began with a segment called "The Gospel According to Whom?" This piece charged that the National Council of Churches (NCCC), World Council of Churches (WCC), and a number of major Protestant denominations are inappropriately involved in political activity around the world, including of armed revolution.[6]

In a news release issued the following day, top Officials of the NCCC denounced the segment as distorted, sensational and biased, and denied the allegations.

As I was working for the New York State Council of Churches, I learned that I was to also serve on the Board of the National Council of Churches. In a July 23, 1981, letter from Rev. Frederick R. Wilson, then the associate general director for Ecumenical and Interchurch Relations of the former Program Agency of the United Presbyterian Church in the USA, I was informed that the 193rd meeting of the General Assembly elected me to serve as a member of the Presbyterian delegation on the Governing Board of the National Council of Churches for the triennium 1982–84. This would be my first time on this Governing Board.

These were real formative years for me with regard to social witness policy formation and application. I saw this as having an opportunity to deal with systems that could alleviate poverty and injustice. Once I said yes to the position and indicated my willingness to move from the Roxbury section of Boston to Albany, NY, little did I know at the time that my first advocacy discussion would be just after I began the job. I was asked by the director to speak with a woman on the legislative committee who thought it was wrong to offer this job as the director of the Albany Office to a woman because I would be taking a job away from a man who needed it to support his family. Over lunch, I assured her that as a single mother, I needed the job to support my family.

Death Penalty: And the Crucifixion

"You shall not murder."
—Exodus 20:13

The most memorable item during my time as the advocate for the justice policies of the thirty-three Protestant and Orthodox denominational members of the New York State Council of Churches was the work against the reestablishment of the death penalty in New York State. Our mantra was, *"Why kill people, who kill people to show that killing people is wrong."* We also presented the growing knowledge that the death penalty was not a deterrent to future crimes.

State Senator William T. Smith from the Forty-Ninth District of Utica, advocated for the use of the death penalty because he said even Christ would support it as evidenced by the fact that he allowed himself to be "executed" on the cross with criminals! This comment surely shows that if we as the church and as individuals do not speak for ourselves, then others will speak for us!

My office let the churches of New York State know how he was supporting his position to re-institute capital punishment in New York State. Church leaders, pastors, and lay people from all over New York State contacted the senator to let him know the true meaning of Christ death on the cross—an action that was to carry our sins on the cross with him. Not an action to show governments how to execute people and that it was okay to do so.

At the time, he was identified as a member of the Catholic Church. We particularly made sure that state Catholic bishops knew what he was saying about the meaning of the crucifixion and its purpose. We encouraged the bishops and other church leaders to visit him and to renew church teachings with him.

He served in the state senate from 1963 until 1986. His 2010 obituary says that he became a member of Big Flats Presbyterian Church. Either he was never really a Catholic or he left it after this controversy to find likeminded Christians. In either case, he never used that argument again. It is not unusual for a politician to find a religious setting that is more suitable to their own understanding of God.

My work with the Council was the director of the Albany Office and of what was then called New York State *Impact*, a legislative advocacy newsletter. This office was in the First Presbyterian Church, just a few blocks from the capital. The main office for the Council was in Syracuse, New York, along with the Synod of the Northeast for the Presbyterian Church.

Casino Gambling: Mistaken for Prostitute

New York was considering bringing legalized gambling to the state as a way to raise revenue. There were bills introduced in the state legislature to legalize it because the neighboring state of New Jersey now had it in Atlantic City as a revenue producer. I was dispatched to that city to learn more about it to see how it might be impacting the churches and the people of the community.

The Council of Representatives, the NY State Council's governing body, determined that we should advocate against it as we referred to the practice as "legalized" gambling. It was characterized this way as we had to distinguish it from "recreational" gambling. Some churches did have bingo. Making this distinction helped to broaden our base of church support.

When I checked into the hotel and gave my credit card for a two-night stay, the clerk seemed a bit baffled. Surprised by the credit card, he handled it in a modest way. I did not know why at first. But I later learned that many of the hotels were used to women checking in only for the hourly rate with cash.

It did not matter that I was dressed in my "lobbyist"-type business suit because they were accustomed to well-dressed women checking in and conducting their "business." In fact, as I later interviewed people, I learned that students came from as far away as Philadelphia and other places to earn money to pay college tuition! So Andrew and Simon, your nana was once suspected of carrying out prostitution!

Such stories meant that the churches had real questions about the impact this industry would have on them and their members. Those who supported it called it gaming. Those who opposed it called it gambling. With jobs being scarce, church members would find jobs in the casinos. Indirectly, contributions from the gambling would come to the churches.

There were other questions dealing with casino chips in the collection plate. Does the pastor, trustee, or elder take them in to be cashed? Should they allow their parking lot to be rented out to casino patrons? In the end, NY did not institute casino gambling at that time.

1980: White House Conference on Families: Governor Hugh Carey Appointment

Dear Reverend Ivory:

I am pleased to appoint you as a delegate to the June, 1980 White House Conference on Families. Congratulations and, on behalf of all of New York's families, thank you for your willingness to serve.

The 123-member New York State delegation assumes the responsibility for expressing the critical concerns of our State's families at the White House Conference and for helping to shape policies which will address those concerns. The delegation, representing the diversity which makes our state so culturally rich and unique, is well equipped to discharge that responsibility.

New Yorkers are looking to you to speak out for them in Baltimore. You take with you my best wishes for success and my commitment that this

*administration will do all it can to further your
efforts to strengthen family life in the 1980's.*

*Sincerely,
Hugh L. Carey
March 20, 1980*

July 1, 1982: Invitation to Unification
Church Mass Wedding

"Indeed, all who want to live a godly life in
Christ Jesus will be persecuted."
—2 Timothy 3:12

In my ecumenical role for churches of New York State, I received an invitation to attend the July wedding for 2,075 couples in Madison Square Garden, New York City.[7] I did not attend.

The Rev. Sun Myung Moon presided over a wedding in Seoul, Korea, as some ten thousand couples wed there. I add this information to this memoir as a little tidbit to show how interesting ecumenism can be. There were those who participated as a way of renewing their wedding vows. Others were matched by the Unification Church without knowing each other ahead of time. As a way of promoting world peace and unity among the races, the couples were of mixed races.

**Lee Jin-man/AP
View Caption**

The Christian Science Monitor entitled it with the question, "Is mass wedding the last for Unification Church's Sun Myung Moon?"

There was a serious side to my involvement with this group, in that the New York State Legislature had regular bills introduced that would have labeled this religion a cult and bring prosecutions to this faith group if any young people became members against their parents' wishes. These bills were called "Deprogramming Bills."

The NY State Council of Churches had the unenviable responsibility of telling the legislature that the US Constitution had a First Amendment Freedom of Religion clause, which gives individuals the right to practice faith as they saw fit. So the Unification Church looked favorability upon us.

In the 1980s, the Unification Church founded in Korea in 1954 was seen as a new religion and viewed with suspicion by traditional and historic religion. Suspicion of new religions has always been a factor within societies around the world.

The United Nations promotes tolerance for religion and freedom from persecution based on one's religion, in Article 18 of the Universal Declaration on Human Rights. It states,

> *Everyone has the right to freedom of thought, conscience and religion; this right includes freedom to change his religion or belief, and freedom, either alone or in community with others and in public or private, to manifest his religion or belief in teaching, practice, worship and observance.*

As Christians, we know from the ministry of the Apostle Paul that we will sometimes be persecuted for professing our faith and beliefs. This is all the more reason to recognize the persecution of others despite the fact that their religion and faith stance may be antithetical to our own.

New York State Passage of Equal Rights Amendment: Governor Mario Cuomo Press Conference

We won!

TIMES UNION   Albany, N.Y., Thursday, June 21, 1984   ;B;5

United Press International
DRAWS SMILES — Members of women's groups smile at a comment by Gov. Mario M. Cuomo at a press conference Wednesday for passage of a state Equal Rights Amendment. Behind the governor, Edward Cleary, state AFL-CIO president, offered additional support.

Child Abuse Prevention Task Force: First Lady Letter

After leaving New State and the Council of Churches position, I headed to Washington, DC. I sent a letter of resignation from the Child Abuse Prevention Task Force to New York State First lady, Ms. Matilda Raffa Cuomo. I served on the task force as the statewide representative for the NY State Council of Churches. Since we do not always expect such recognition to follow us, I thought I would print the contents of her brief letter here, as sent to what was then my new Georgia Avenue, MD address:

> Dear Elenora,
> *I have just learned that you have relocated to Washington, D.C. to assume new responsibilities for the Presbyterian Church. We will miss your energetic*

and thoughtful contributions to our work on child abuse prevention and other key social concerns.

On behalf of your colleagues on the Child Abuse Prevention Task Force and the Clergy Coalition, our deepest appreciation for all that you have contributed to our efforts and our best wishes for the future.

Yours Sincerely,
Matilda R. Cuomo
September 13, 1985

8

47

Part 4

1985–1989: National Capital Presbytery: Associate for Mission and Ecumenical Affairs

Presidency of Ronald Reagan and George H. W. Bush

"I was sick and you took care of me . . ."
—Matthew 25:36

When AIDS was on the front pages of the news stories, I represented the Presbytery on the board of the Interfaith Conference of Metropolitan (IFC) Washington, as it wrestled with how to respond to this epidemic with the growing number of worldwide deaths. IFC currently has ten major faith groups among its membership—Baha'i, Buddhist, Hindu-Jain, Islamic, Jewish, Latter-Day Saints, Protestant, Roman Catholic, Sikh, and Zoroastrian. The most challenging concern to the general society and particularly to the religious community at that time was the development and spreading of the virus of AIDS. The question was posed to the Board—"*Should the religious leadership say something about this to its membership?*"

In the 1980s, the AIDS virus was thought by some to be a punishment from God and a sin that should be punished and sufferers should not be made welcome in church, mosque, temple, or synagogue. It was seen as a gay man's disease and should be shunned.

It was at this time, in the early 1980s, that religious leaders began to help their members understand that AIDS was not a punishment from God and that it was not casually passed on from one person to the next. Those who were the victims of this virus deserved

51

our compassion and welcome as children of God. I was happy to be part of the IFC as it came to an understanding of kindheartedness.

1982: The Baptism, Eucharist, and Ministry Report (BEM) of the World Council of Churches (WCC)

"This famous text, adopted by Faith and Order at its plenary commission meeting in Lima, Peru in 1982, explores the growing agreement - and remaining differences - in fundamental areas of the churches' faith and life. The most widely-distributed and studied ecumenical document, BEM has been a basis for many "mutual recognition" agreements among churches and remains a reference today."

This report was released to the churches of the world in a press release dated January 15, 1982. It can still be found on the WCCC website. It was extremely controversial because of several ascertain. My task as the associate at the Presbytery was to respond to questions about it from our local churches. I remember setting up a session for clergy and lay to come into the office to discuss it.

Some people came wanting to tear it down and have us disassociated from the WCCC. One such detractor went on and on over the phone until I told him that the Presbytery level was not where the decision was made to support and present this document to Presbyterian churches. The decision to distribute the report came from our national offices and the ecumenical officer there after approval from the General Assembly of the PC(USA)s highest governing board. He still kept going on and on negatively about it. I pulled out my directory and gave him the name of Rev. Lew Lancaster, who was in the office responsible for it. He suddenly stopped. He said is, "Lew supporting this? Are you sure?"

I said, "Yes. Our copies came to us through his office with the encouragement to have our churches in National Capital Presbytery study it."

Again, he said, "Lew Lancaster? Well if Lew supports it, it must be okay." He then said good-bye and I never heard from him again. This shows how sometimes, even in the church, it depends on who you know and who knows you.

What I remember most about the report is that it said that you do not always need bread to celebrate communion. Bread and wheat are not always readily available to everyone around the world. Sometimes rice will do just as well to convey that it is just the symbol of sacrifice, brokenness, and forgiveness that is in the shared cup and the shared life-sustaining grain that we bring to the common sacramental table. Amen.

October 19–November 9, 1986: South America Mission Study Seminar

A twelve-inch doll made of black cotton fabric and wearing a pink hat with a yellow red-flowered dress was given to me after I preached Sunday morning service at Igreja *Presbiteriana Unida do Parque Acavii.* A young woman in the congregation ran all the way back to her house from the church to bring it to me before our group left for the airport as we headed on the next leg of our journey. She said that I reminded her of the doll she made, and she wanted me to have it. She took the time to include a note in Spanish, which said,

> *(Espera no senhoe anima-te, eele foetaleccia o teu coracao. sal 27 14) or "Wait on the Lord, cheer up and he will strengthen your heart" (Psalm 27:14).* It concluded with *"igieja que ama vocee" (Church that loves you.)*

I knew ahead of time that I was expected to deliver the sermon on that morning. Since each word I uttered would have to be translated, I prepared something brief using the Ten Commandments of Exodus 20 and coupled with that poem, *"All I need to know, I learned in kindergarten"* by Rev. Robert Fulghum.[10] Basically, I wanted to convey the message of our traveling seminar that we need to get to know those of other cultures and how can we live among one another in peace and respect.

There were twenty participants on this trip, which included the leader, Rev. Benjamin F. Gutierrez, who was the Liaison Latin America/Caribbean at the 475 Riverside Drive, New York offices of the General Assembly. It was put together as a young pastor's tour for those under the age of forty. I slipped in as I had just turned forty-one.

The group was a deliberate blend of both North American clergy, Central and South American Clergy. We started out speaking three continually translated languages at all times—English, Spanish, and Mam, a dialect of Guatemala. There were also two Portuguese speakers in group.

Our North American group of nine was male and female— white, black, Hispanic, and one Korean women pastor, Rev. In Sook Lee. Rev. Lee, whose native language was Korean, sometimes had trouble understanding English when it was spoken with a Spanish accent and sat close to me so that I could repeat what was said.

We rehearsed how to introduce ourselves in both languages so that each time we made a stop at a new place, the people there would come to understand that we were serious about really getting to know them and to know their story.

The Latin American participants of our seminar group were from Mexico, Guatemala, Costa Rica, Uruguay, and Brazil. There was only one woman in this group. She was not ordained clergy.

> *"In a report back to the wider church about this trip on December 9, 1986 we read," The Presbyterian Church (U.S.A.) and the Asociacion de Iglesisas Presbiterianas y Reformadas en America Latina (AIPRAL—the Association of Presbyterian and Reformed Churches in Latin America) co-sponsored a mission study seminar to South America recently. For three weeks, from October 19 to November 9, participants from six countries traveled and studied the life and ministry of the Church in Brazil, Uruguay and Argentina ... Such diversity was both cumbersome and enriching. Everything had to be translated at least three times (in multiple directions'). Participants had to pay attention more, closely and be patient with each another!*

One sensitive point came when the South Americans realized that the North Americans were told not to drink the South American water and that we needed bottled water and drinks. We explained that people often have sensitivities to different waters and if they came to the US, our water might upset their stomachs also. I think this explanation worked to settle that tension down. Along the way, I learned to order a *cerveza* to keep the stomach settled. This was a light beer.

This is a picture of part of the group as we waited to board a bus to our next destination.

11

The seminar had a focus for each visited county that included religion and culture—ecumenism in Latin America; ecclesial, social, economic, and political realities in Latin America today; historical elements of these realities; and the role and witness of the Church in these realities. Much of the focus came from direct experience.

In addition to the experience at the Church, I was impressed to see how the African-Brazilians were able to hold onto their culture, even though they, too, had been brought there in enslavement. You could see it in the street vendors who were selling their food:

12

As our group traveled south from northern South America stopping in Bahia, Rio de Janeiro, and San Palo, Brazil, and onto places in Montevideo, Uruguay, and Buenos Aries, Argentina, I could not help but think of the similarities you have as you travel from the southern parts of the east coast of the United States to our northern parts up in Vermont and Maine. It felt as though the closer you are to the equator, the more African ethnic the people seem to be. It was as though you put the palms of your hands together and spread them out as you image the United States south and the South American north being near your wrist. As you move upward and outward toward the tips of your fingers, the people become whiter. In the passing thirty-plus years, this may have changed.

When I returned to the US and shared information about my trip with some of the churches that invited me to speak, I told them that I learned about the "extermination squads" that take it upon themselves to kill street children who live in the alleys and on door-steps. One man vehemently called me a liar. This could not be true. I must have been making it up. It is hard to believe. These children live on the streets without supervision or they spend all day and night begging from tourist.

For this essay, I Googled "Brazilian children killed in the streets" and immediately found this story: http://articles.latimes.com/1990-07-08/news/mn-324_1_death-squads.

The legacy of slavery's racism still holds within the culture. Even in the church-related buildings, as the black people entered through the back door to do the work of cleaning and serving. Those who entered were surprised that I could come into the front door. I no longer have it, but I once had an article that explained how the type of hair you have also determines your statues in Brazil, if your skin color is borderline too dark.

Part 5

1989–2007: Washington Office of the Presbyterian Church (USA)

Presidency of George H. W. Bush, Bill Clinton, and George W. Bush

"Seek good and not evil, that you may live; and so the LORD, the God of hosts, will be with you, just as you have said. Hate evil and love good, and establish justice in the gate; it may be that the LORD, the God of hosts, will be gracious to the remnant of Joseph."

—Amos 5:14–15

I saw the eighteen years of advocacy justice work in the Washington Office of the Presbyterian Church as the fulfillment of this Amos passage. The Office was there to stand at the "gates of injustice" and let all who would listen know that the Lord would have us all implement justice.

Over the years, many people have heard me say in sermons, plenary speeches, workshops, and writings that, like the prophet Amos, we must challenge even the head priest in the temple, if they were not fighting for justice.

The head priest during the time of Amos was Amaziah. He complained to the government authorities about the work Amos was trying to do.

Then Amaziah, the priest of Bethel, sent to King Jeroboam of Israel, saying, "Amos has conspired against you in the very center of the house of Israel; the land is not able to bear all his words."

And Amaziah said to Amos, "O seer, go flee away to the land of Judah, earn your bread there, and prophesy there but never again prophesy at Bethel, for it is the king's sanctuary, and it is a temple of the kingdom."

Then Amos answered Amaziah, "I am no prophet, nor a prophet's son; but I am a herdsman, and a dresser of sycamore trees, and the LORD *took me from following the flock, and the* LORD *said to me, Go, prophesy to my people Israel."' (Amos 5)*

The Washington Office was established in 1946 to do just what Amos was talking about. And yes, there were modern-day Priest Amaziah, who said that neither the church nor the nation *"is able to bear all its words."* Even though these were words that came from the General Assembly, yet I heard someone in power say that just because the General Assembly said it, it does not mean that we have to repeat it. I for one had always taken the General Assembly and its justice policies seriously.

And so it went. There were constant challenges from the conservative corners of the church and lead by the publication called the *Layman.*[13] The Washington Office and I became their main target. My portfolio on issues impacting women, race, religious freedom, immigration, and criminal justice served as lightning rods for these attacks.

I served as the first director of the reunited church office. The mandate of Rev. George Chauncy, who served in the former Southern Presbyterian Office based in Atlanta, was to have been the "communicator" back to the churches but not to "lobby" in Washington. On the other hand, Ms. Mary Jane Paterson, as she served the New York City based Northern stream Washington Office, was tasked to speak to elected officials in the name of the church.

When I was hired in 1989, I succeeded both of them as the offices had been combined during the reunion of the two churches that once split over the issue of slavery more than one hundred years before—one church supporting slavery and the other opposing it.

In my speaking, before I began to actually touch on some of the controversial issues, I usually told a short modern-day parable that I used a lot over the last forty years of social justice ministry. I first heard it from a Catholic priest so I have not changed it very much.

The parable begins with a priest and a recent convert to religion, walking along a riverbank in a country where the church is growing very fast with new converts to the membership. The priest and the recent convert are talking with much joy about the convert's newly found faith, when they look over into the river and see someone floating. They reach in, pull the person out, and administer emergency first aid. The person is revived and goes on his way. The priest turns to the recent convert and asked, "Isn't it great that our faith allowed us to be here during this time of need?" The recent convert said yes.

On the second day, the priest and the recent convert were walking along the same riverbank and again talking about the newly found faith of the convert, when they saw a few people floating down the river. They pulled them out and called for medical help because they needed more than quick riverbank first aid. They were taken to the hospital that had been paid for by our mission dollars. These people were treated and released. The priest again asked the recent convert, "Isn't it great that our faith allowed us to be there during a time of need?" The convert again said yes.

And yes again, on the third day, they walked and talked along the riverbank. This time there were more bodies. The priest and the recent convert pulled these people out too. More people of faith got involved with the rescue. The priest asked the recent convert again, "Isn't it great tht our faith allowed us to be here during this time of need?"

This time, the recent convert looked at the priest and asked, "Why don't we go to the top of the river, find out what is happening, and stop it?" Once the recent convert asked that question, it became an issue of establishing justice at the gates of injustice at the top of the river from which the bodies were flowing.

aff of the Presbyterian Washington Office on the steps of the U.S. Supreme Court: *top row, left to* *jht,* Henry Hammock, Douglas Grace, Walter Owensby; *middle row,* Bernadine McRipley, Elenora iddings Ivory, Barbara Green; *bottom row,* Cathy Sunshine and Sariah Knight

There are some who may say that the priest and the recent convert should keep their ministry local and not get involved in whatever systems or situations caused those bodies to come floating down the river. To stay at the riverbank where the bodies are floating is important. Staying there is providing direct and immediate service, and it is important. This is the Good Samaritan story, as told in three Gospels: Luke 10:25–37, Matthew 22:34–40, Mark 12:28–34.

Some would say that it is enough for the religious community to be the good Samaritans of direct service ministries, to do charitable works as a primary focus. Others would say charity is not enough in and of itself. We need to stop the injuries and violence and oppression before people become victims. We need to go to the top of the river to the gates where the injustice is taking place. This is to address the systemic change that the recent convert was asking about. I understand public policy as working toward systemic change.

It is not a new thing for people of faith to hear from church leaders and members that it may not be the appropriate time to speak to politics and that the best mode is to work on direct services instead. The Priest Amaziah still lives today in many of our churches. He still says that the land and the church are not able to hear the words of Amos.

These people would respond to the recent convert in the parable above by telling him that they should stay at the point of the river where the bodies are floating down and to not go to attempt to stop whatever is happening.

To challenge government authority is still an uneasy proposition to many in the faith community. However, if you are from one of the oppressed communities such as people of color or minority faith groups, you have come to know that you have to stand up for what you believe and ask for fairness. Jesus did not spend his days on whatever the equivalent of a golf course would have been in those days. Jesus spent his days with the poor and afflicted.

Without going into too much depth with too many issues, I have selected a few particular topics here below from my time on Capitol Hill. By remembering that Justice Advocates, both clergy and lay, do not see justice issues as being binary to either the secular realm or the religious realm. I like to say that justice is not either liberal or conservative; right or left republican or democrat. Justice is just justice.

Look at the judgment of the nations in Matthew 25:31–46, where we see that they shall be judged by the way they treat their poor. The issues below are in chronological order. They will begin to address health care, poverty, women's rights, and even forgiveness of a president of the United States for his transgressions.

June 1991: Christian Responsibility and a National Medical Plan

"I needed clothes and you clothed me, I was sick and you looked after me, I was in prison and you came to visit me.' 'Truly I tell you, whatever you did for one of the least of these brothers and sisters of mine, you did for me.'"
—Mathew 25:36, 40

As I write this essay, I am watching the June 22, 2017 television coverage of a demonstration outside the Senate offices of Mitch

McConnell the Senate Republican Majority leader over the intro-
duction of many of several bills that are designed to overturn and
diminish the Affordable Care Act, also known as Obamacare. People
with disabilities have descended on the capitol to voice opposition
against projected reduction of this funding of health care for those
without insurance. It is painful to watch people in wheelchairs being
pushed out by the capitol police. I would not want their jobs.

In 1990, the Washington Offices of the denominations launched
a revised joint advocacy effort to urge the federal government to provide health care to children who did not have it. This was really a
re-launch, because the offices had covered this in the past, but could
not get real results. The General Assembly had been speaking to this
issue since 1946. The aim was to get children covered, those with
preexisting conditions, those without employer provided health care
and women's wide-ranging health care needs.

We organized a press conference. Reporters attended, but they
stated that they did not understand what the problem was. *"Who
would not want everyone to have health care?"* they asked.

This was clearly one of those times when society, in general,
did not really understand the problem. Of course, everyone supports
health care, but not everyone agrees with the solution. You could say
that the "devil is in the details." After we explained the justice side of
the health issue, in that Jesus explained that not caring for the poor
is not caring for Him, we told the press that they needed to look
at the money side of health care to understand fully. We then told
them what the business side of the health care industry would be
concerned about, if a Medicare for all or a single-payer program were
adopted, it could put current insures out of business or reduce their
bottom line. There was also the states' rights argument. Is health care
a state responsibility or a national one?

Once the media came to understand the financial side of health
care, they then had a controversy that could be reported. This took
place in the early days of the Clinton administration, with Hillary
Clinton as the lead from the Whitehouse and Senator Ted Kennedy
in the Senate. We worked with both offices and had many meetings
with the lead offices.

The late Rev. Bernadine Grant McRipley was our lead staff person from the Presbyterian office. As much as we would have liked getting a single-payer health care system, meaning that we all would be in a Medicare type system, we knew we would not get that far. We were discussing whether health care is a privilege, but not a right. If health care is a privilege, then not everyone should expect to get it—least of all from government. Therefore, do not even think of realistically advocating for a single-payer system.

We reminded anyone who would listen that Social Security started small and was amended and expanded over the years to include things like supplemental security for the poor—SSI. There are still those who fight to discontinue Social Security.

May 17, 1995: Christian Coalition's Contract with the American Family

"When the Son of Man comes in his glory, and all the angels with him, then he will sit on the throne of his glory. All the nations will be gathered before him, and he will separate people one from another as a shepherd separates the sheep from the goats, and he will put the sheep at his right hand and the goats at his left."

—Matthew 25:31–33

The Christian Coalition was a strong conservative force during the 1990s. Wikipedia gives it this description,

The Contract with America was a document released by the United States Republican Party during the 1994 Congressional election campaign. Written by Newt Gingrich and Dick Armey, and in part using text from former President Ronald Regan's 1985 State of the Union Address, the Contract detailed the actions the Republicans promised to take if they became the majority party in the United States House of Representatives for the first time in 40 years. Many of the Contract's policy ideas originated at The Heritage Foundation, a conservative think tank.[1][2]

The Contract with America was introduced six weeks before the 1994 Congressional election, the first mid-term election of President Bill Clinton's Administration, and was signed by all but two of the Republican members of the House and all of the Party's non-incumbent Republican Congressional candidates." https://en.wikipedia.org/wiki/Contract_with_America

Lots of energy and explanation was needed to point out that the focus of this "Contract" was not beneficial for low income families. It would have brought about intrusion into freedom of religion regarding where we pray; public funds diverted to private sectarian schools; imposing one theological view of reproductive choice and stark reduction of public economic support for the poor.

Our entre to the White House at the time was through Ms. Flo MacAfee, who was then serving as the liaison with the religious community. Since much acrimony had surfaced due to this proposal, she wanted to know if there was anything the churches could recommend to cool things down and bring some semblance of civility back to Washington. This was perhaps the most difficult question I had ever been asked by a public official. I had to say to her sadly, that we had not quite figured that out within church interactions and have no real solutions for the government. She being an Episcopalian understood this answer as her church was also going through some of the same turmoil as many other denominations were. After a few moments, we just moved on to another topic. I always like to say that a hospital is built for sick people, a cemetery is for dead people, and the church is for sinners. So we, as church people, cannot make claim to having truly responded to the call of Jesus to be at peace with one another.

At the heart of this "Contract" was an interest on the part of a fiscally conservative group in Congress to reduce the size of government at all levels and to reduce the spending on poverty programs in particular. They gained enough power to have the federal government shut down. What they and many of their supporters across the country did not understand was that federal government services were not just in Washington with its fancy buildings and marble monuments. They did not think through the fact that the regional Social Security, veterans, regional passport offices, and post offices where indeed federal buildings that were also shut down and they did.

The *Contract with America* debate taught the country that the government is people. Abraham Lincoln, in his November 19, 1863, Gettysburg, Pennsylvania, address stated that it is a "Government of the people, by the people and for the people." That should mean that the wellbeing of the people must be seriously considered.

Those faith groups that advocated against the "Contract" for its shortsightedness, where challenged by some in congress who thought we had no mandate to speak to these issue or any issue. "*What is your authority to speak to us?*" they asked. At least twice I simply copied Matthew 25:31–46 to say that the nation will be judged by the way it treats the "least of these" among us.

During this debate about the "Contract," what may not have been generally known by most people was that Newt Gingrich's Washington, DC, apartment was directly above the Washington Office of the Presbyterian Church in the United Methodist Building. Several other denominational offices and justice advocacy groups were also in that building at 110 and 100 Maryland Avenue NE. Any organizations or elected officials who lived there received the benefit of reduced rents by virtue of the fact that the building was tax exempt. I always thought that this was hypocritical of him to receive the privilege. But it is possible that he was paying above and beyond the regular rent rate or he could have been giving a generous contribution to the United Methodist Church for the privilege of living in their building.

September 4–15, 1995 Beijing: Fourth World Conference on Women Action for Equality, Development, and Peace

First Lady Hillary Rodham Clinton[14] was a keynote speaker. She rocked the world when she said during her presentation that *"Women's rights are human rights."* It may be hard to fathom now, but these words were like a great tsunami hitting the world with the reverberations felt across the globe. The rights for women in the workplace, in the family, and generally in society were to be placed second to the rights of the men who nearly possessed them.

I was there as part of the United States non-governmental (NGO) delegation to what was informally called the Beijing Women's Conference. I was with the religious representatives. More than 189 world governments sent delegations. *"More than 5,000 representatives from 2,100 NGOs and 5,000 media representatives attended the conference and nearly 30,000 individuals attended the independent NGO FORUM '95"*[15]

The event was organized by the Commission on the Status of Women, with the United Nations Division for the Advancement of Women (DAW). Its final document was called the *"Beijing Declaration and Platform for Action."* It was adopted on September 15, 1995, by consensus of the governments attending the Conference. Its goal was to lead the various nations into the advancement of a gender perspective that reflected in all policies and programs improvements for women at the national, regional and international levels.

We can look at the world today and see that movement has happened but there is much, much more that can be done with regard to sexual exploitation, voting rights, workplace fairness among other markers of life's endeavors. Women can now drive in Saudi Arabia, after a long battle to gain that privilege. But the girls captured by the Boko Haram in Nigeria, simply for going to school, is an example that much more still needs to be done. The #MeToo movement around the ending the issues of sexual harassment in the workplace, politics, and schools seems to be just taking off.

And let's not forget our own internal struggles with women's rights. Within our churches, it is still difficult for a woman to be accepted as the senior pastor of a large church or to get a full salary–paying church.

July 23, 1996: Religious Liberty: Prayer in School Testimony: House Committee on the Judiciary Sub-Committee on the Constitution

Each morning, one of my grade school teachers would begin the day by reading one of the Psalms from the Bible. She would sometimes tear the page out of the Bible and then throw it away. I could never understand why she did that, and I did not ask questions. Was she simply marking her page for the next time or was this her disrespect for the Bible. Did she read it only because it was part of her job?

Do we really want to entrust a teacher or any public official with our scared text? When Congress had a bill before them entitled *"Legislation to Further Protect Religious Freedom,"* which was designed to make prayer mandatory in public schools, I was asked to give testimony in the House Sub-Committee on the Judiciary in opposition to this bill at a July 23, 1996, Hearing.

Our General Assembly policy, *"God Alone is Lord of the Conscience,"* would oppose this idea. I had also been asked to deliver a press statement on the steps of the Supreme Court on November 22, 1994, as organized by the religious advocacy community. This was done with other denominations.

Young people already have the freedom to bow their heads and pray over their food, to pray before a test or sports outings in school. They do not need a public official to suggest that. We do not want to open the door to forced coercion of prayers or embarrassing children who may practice a religion that is different from that which is being presented by a teacher or public leader.

We people of faith do not agree on how we recognize or address God, so why should we subject our children to that confusion in public. Some of us stand, some kneel, and some bow their heads. We bring our petitions to God each in our own way and each in our own time.

October 1, 1997: Bell vs. Ivory et al.
United States Court of Appeals, Fourth Circuit

I would not have included this case among these essays, except for the fact that if you ever Google my name, this case might come up. So I thought I would very briefly say something here in this chronological list of events that this document represents.

When the case first came forward at the District of Columbia Court level, it bore the name "Bell v. Ivory." The courts treated it as an ordinary run-of-the-mill labor dispute case. The major parties where clergy of various denominations and the denominations themselves. At dispute was the question, do we, as churches, have the right to determine when to hire and fire and when to stop joint funding of ancillary organizations we may have created?

In our Capitol Hill Advocacy work, the religious organizations created entities where we could work in a unified way on issues of poverty, justice, and peace. Interfaith Impact was just such an organization that we were forced to dismantle for financial reasons. The dismantling was not a reflection on the quality of work done by the hired staff. The need to dismantle was a reflection on the fact that we had fewer funds to carry out this work in this way.

I was the chairperson at the time of this law suit. Our sponsoring denominational organizations had less and less money to fund its own operations let alone fund additional entities that they may have created during more lucrative times.

Since I was the chair and the one who wrote a letter from the PC (USA) Washington Office saying that we could no longer afford to support the organization, I became the lead defendant in this case that bears my name.

James M. BELL, Plaintiff-Appellant, v. PRESBYTERIAN CHURCH (U.S.A.); Board of Church and Society of the United Methodist Church; Women's Division of the General Board of Global Ministries of the United Methodist Church; American Baptist Churches in the U.S.A., Defendants-Appellees, Elenora Giddings Ivory; Jane Hull Harvey; Anna Rhee; Jay Lintner; Robert Tiller; Lionel Derenoncourt; Otis Turner; Vernon Broyles, Defendants.

No. 96-1297. Decided: October 01, 1997

It went before HALL and NIEMEYER, Circuit Judges, and DUFFY, United States District Judge for the District of South Carolina, sitting by designation.

ARGUED: James Bell, the Appellant was represented by, James Wright Crabtree, from the firm Smathers & Thompson, Charlotte, NC,

We were most grateful for our pro bono attorneys Alissa Aaronson Horvitz, and Katharine B. Houlihan, from the firm of Morgan, Lewis & Bockius, L.L.P., Washington, DC,

OPINION: The Reverend James M. Bell, an ordained minister, served as executive director of Interfaith Impact, a multi-denominational outreach program. In June 1995, his employment was terminated as part of Interfaith Impact's "complete reduction in force." Interfaith Impact's board of directors advised Bell that the termination was "based solely upon the financial condition" of the program and was "absolutely no reflection on the quality of your work." Bell sued Interfaith Impact's four principal constituent religious organizations, as well as others, for breach of contract and various torts arising from the termination. The district court dismissed the complaint against the constituent religious organizations because of a lack of subject matter jurisdiction, concluding that, by reason of the First Amendment, a civil court has no jurisdiction over ecclesiastical decisions by churches "as to how they are going to expend their funds." For the reasons that follow, we affirm the judgment of the district court.[16]

June 1998: House Judiciary Committee Testimony
Religious Liberty Protection Act of 1998[17]
"God Alone Is Lord of the Conscience"

This concern started with the desire of the International Monetary Fund (IMF), commonly known as the World Bank that wanted to acquire the property next door in order to expand their facilities. It happened to be where Western Presbyterian Church was located for many years. Western was first organized in 1855, Washington, DC.

In addition to its regularly scheduled Sunday morning worship services, among other ministries, the church had a feeding program called Miriam's Kitchen for the homeless—many of whom lived on the surrounding streets. Their website says that "By early 1984, Miriam's Kitchen was feeding more than 200 homeless men and women a hot, nutritious breakfast five days a week in the church basement." "After all, Jesus said, when I was hungry, you fed me."

> *As our ministry with the homeless grew, so did our membership. At the same time, our next-door neighbor the International Monetary Fund needed property to expand its offices. After two years of negotiating with the fund, Western signed an agreement that paid for us to construct a new church on the corner of Virginia Avenue at 24th and G Streets and provided a significant endowment for mission work in exchange for the old property on H Street.*
>
> *The IMF purchased the old property and moved the church brick by brick to the new location. "The*

move sparked conflict with some neighborhood residents who didn't want Miriam's Kitchen feeding the homeless at the new church. City politicians sided with those who didn't want Miriam's Kitchen in Foggy Bottom, and Western pursued the issue in court."

"Our immediate neighborhood is a part of Washington's Northwest quadrant known as Foggy Bottom. It stretches from the John F. Kennedy Performing Arts Center to Rock Creek Park to Georgetown, to Pennsylvania Avenue NW, to 17th Street to Constitution Avenue. Within these boundaries are the White House and Executive Office Building, the Watergate complex, St. Mary's Senior Apartments, and numerous other apartment buildings within walking distance of the church."

When Western moved their outreach to the homeless to this highly upscale neighborhood, they met with opposition that claimed that they had out reached their ministry purpose, in that in their minds, the proper work of the church, any church, should be restricted to Sunday morning.

Churches were no longer seen as good neighbors. Churches have come to be seen as taking up parking with their weekday programing and Sunday worship. Churches brought in "undesirables" with their outreach programs.

A part of my coalitional efforts through my position as the director of the Washington Office was to work with denominations on issues of Religious Liberty. Western Presbyterian was one of the concerns the interreligious coalition discussed. The Coalition was made up of Jews, Muslims, Christians, Sikhs, etc. All had concern about the government determination about the parameters of what makes legitimate ministry in their minds.

The coalition wanted to gather as much information as possible in order to approach Congress and develop legislation that would protect ministry programs based on the freedom of religion found in the First Amendment of the Constitution.

I offered to have a question asked of all of our 11,500+ congregations during the annual Stated Clerk questionnaire sent to all congregations with the obligation to complete. The question asked,

> *Since January 1, 1992, has your congregation needed any form or permit from a government authority that regulates the use of land? These authorities include zoning boards, planning commissions, landmark commissions, and (sometimes) city/county councils?*

The response indicated that dealing with neighbors and local governments had become problematic in some locations. The coalition was scheduled to give testimony on all of our findings and concerns. I was to present our PC (USA) findings and testimony to the Judiciary Committee of the House of Representatives during a hearing. We went to support the bill that was designed to protect church ministries, called the *Religious Freedom Restoration Act (RFRA)*.

RFRA also went to the Senate but did not pass there, thus failing to become law. It failed primarily because there was disagreement between the religious liberty and civil rights advocates.

A more focused bill was introduced and passed in both houses called *"Religious Land Use and Institutionalized Persons Act of 2000 (RLUAIPA)."* This was a compromise between those who have primary concern for religious liberty and those who hold primary concern for civil rights issues. This bill focused narrowly on land use cases and those cases of institutionalized persons.

This was seen as one of those real victories. It was much needed. But all through the working of the Coalition to get RFRA and later RLUAIPA, I worried that there would be some individuals and groups that would use them to deny minority and women's rights by claiming a religious privilege for a particular discrimination against women or a minority.

My fears have been realized as Hobby Lobby claims religious privilege to not give employers reproductive health care as part of their insurance. And situations were a bakery shop claimed religious privilege to avoid making a wedding cake for a gay couple. If the Supreme Court finds in favor of a baker to deny making a cake for a gay couple can he also refuse to make a cake for an interracial couple as well? RFRA and RLUAIPA were not meant to be used for discriminatory purposes.

September 11, 1998:
White House Prayer Breakfast

"From the Bible John 8.7 where Jesus tells the accusers of a woman of adultery, He that is without sin among you, let him first cast a stone at her."

I thought this was one of the ordinary occasionally scheduled White House Prayer Breakfast. Religious leaders from the major faith groups were invited through the office of the White House Social Secretary Ms. Ann Stock. I was seated next to her at the breakfast. After an opening prayer and the serving of our eggs, muffins, and coffee, President Bill Clinton rose to the podium to welcome those present and thank them for attending.

What happened next was unexpected. The country was in the midst of the crises of his presidency involving the inappropriate sexual relationship with Monica Lewinsky. His wife, First Lady Hilary Rodham Clinton, stood by him at the time, as she said she believed his denial.

President Clinton had already appeared on the CBS *60 Minutes* news program. He had already looked straight into the camera on August 17, 1998, and told the public that *"I did not have sex with that woman."*

By the day of the breakfast, his public denials had unraveled and began to have less credibility. Incredibly, during this entire time, it appeared that the White House and the government seemed to go on as usual without distraction from this scandal. Those of us Capitol Hill advocates also went about our issue advocacy as usual since the issues of justice needed promotion—support for welfare, against the death penalty, and following the Central America wars and turmoil, etc.

As President William Jefferson Clinton rose to the podium, we did not expect him to admit his guilt and then to go on to speak to us as religious leaders. He petitioned to us as clergy, Jewish, Muslim, Catholic, Protestant, to ask for forgiveness for his sin against his family, against duties as president and against the country. So there we were, being called on as he evoked the forgiveness from God through all who were present. These breakfasts are usually about us hearing a public policy item or two the president wants to bring forward to Congress and in enlisting our help to get it going. We likewise would have an opportunity to say what is important to the religious community. These breakfasts are not generally about family matters and personal shortcomings.

I do not remember the exact number of us who were present, but I would guess the approximately one hundred of us sat silently as the breakfast came to an end. I did not know what to say to others at my table. As I remember, there was little conversation. Among those clergy present, was Dr. Philp Wogaman who was the pastor of the Foundry Methodist Church where the Clinton's worshiped during their time in Washington.

As was my usual practice, I wrote a short reflection of the event and sent it out to the Washington Office e-mailing list. Of course, it garnered lots of attention within the Church, but also in the country as the secular newspapers and TV news programs wrote stories about this public confession. The press was in the breakfast room with their

designed to avoid and why it is time to lift the burden of fifty years of bad economic decisions that have created the present debt crises.

Religious groups, such as the Episcopal Church, United Methodist, United Church of Christ, the US Catholic Conference, the National Council of Churches, the Union of American Hebrew Congregations, Friends Committee on National Legislation (Quakers) as well as our own Presbyterian Church (USA), came together in coalition with labor groups, development organizations and environmental coalitions over the issue of forgiveness of debt owed to the rich nation of the US by some of poorer world nations.

In God's envisioned world, no person, no family, and by extension, no nation is to be permanently impoverished. Oppressive debt is like peonage. Peonage is never an acceptable result of debt. Economic relationships are never to be allowed to make life hopeless. With debt relief, we have faced up to the reality that most of the debt of the poorest countries will not and cannot be repaid.

The poorest countries around the globe are being paralyzed in their self-development by an unbearable debt load accumulated over decades. Until now, borrowers and lenders alike have procrastinated in facing the reality that much of this debt cannot be repaid—at least not without imposing morally unacceptable levels of sacrifice on innocent people. The ordinary people of these impoverished countries—primarily the women and children—suffer great deprivation as their governments slash education, health, transportation, sanitation, and subsistence programs while orienting their economies ever more toward exports to generate funds toward debt repayment. This repayment has required unconscionable human sacrifice that falls heavily on the most vulnerable people in these debtor nations.

Until this debt is removed, indebted nations will continue being unable to spend even minimally necessary amounts on safe drinking water and other essential services. Only major shifts in national economies will alter those realities, and only ending the burden of crushing debt will make such changes possible.

To those who would say the United States and other nations should not support debt relief, I would say that it would be an act of injustice to not move forward. Debt relief is an act of justice. It is not to be put in political terms. Justice is not liberal or conservative. Justice is not left or right, democratic or republican—*justice* is just justice. It is about fairness. Fairness is God's message to us all. As we celebrate our nation's increased prosperity and that of many of the other developed nations around the world, we must remember that not all nations have experienced this prosperity due to long held past debts that are held by the prosperous nations.

The Bible tells us that "to whom much is given much is expected" (Luke 12:48). The religious principles of many of us here today would dictate that much is expected of us when it comes to the poor. This is particularly true, if some action of our own has worked toward creating this increasing debt of interest payments due—upon more interest payments that are past due.

Enough is enough! For every month's delay to forgive the debt, thousands of lives are lost that might be saved by freeing these nations to be able to spend their money on food, medicine, and inoculations instead of making payments on international debts. Whatever the intent or purpose of our past economic policies may have been, their result has been to make life harder for the poor majorities in these societies in order to transfer money to wealthy nations and the international financial institutions that represent their interests.

The purpose of debt relief is to stand with those nations who have high levels of human need, environmental distress, and are unable to meet the needs of those the Bible refers to as "the least of these" (Matthew 25:31–40). The Washington Office staff associates who worked on this issue of international economic justice was first Walter Owensby until his retirement and then Catherine Gordon.

In his remarks, President Clinton said, *"I have committed our nation during my service as President to wage an intensified battle against global poverty. I never accepted the idea that millions have to be left behind while the rest of us move ahead. By lifting the weakest, poorest among us, we lift all the rest of us, as well. I hope that this idea will be a priority in our foreign policy for a long time to come, no less important than promoting trade, investment and financial stability."*

Our focus in 2000 was on international debt relief; little did we know that in 2017, we would be faced with the debt relief question with regard to Puerto Rico following Hurricane Irma. Should they receive aid is questioned in some quarters because they are in debt. Although they will be without electrical power for months, is this the right time to ask such a question of anybody, but particularly other Americans? Aren't we supposed to assist the poor? *"Blessed are they who hunger and thirst for righteousness, for they shall be satisfied"* (*Matthew 5*).

September 11, 2001 (9/11): Return No One Evil for Evil

The congregational charge and benediction I usually give at the end of a worship service where I have preached can be found in the PC (USA) worship book—

> *Go out into the world in Peace, have courage, return no one evil for evil, support the weak, honor all persons, love and serve the Lord, while rejoicing in the power of the Holy Spirit—The grace of our Lord Jesus Christ and the Communion of the Holy Spirit be with us all—now and forever more—Amen.*

Beginning on the first Sunday after the planes hit the Twin Towers in New York, the Pentagon in Washington, DC, and the open fields in Pennsylvania, these words were hard for some of us to hear and follow. I like to say that there is no easy button that comes with the Bible. After the attack, there was an immediate sense of wanting the nation to retaliate, if we could figure out exactly who to take revenge upon.

The attacks were on the second Tuesday morning of September when our regularly scheduled Witness in Washington issue briefings would have been held at 10:00 a.m. It was a very bright and warm day. The office windows were open. We could hear something loud as the plane crashed into the Pentagon. We saw the planes crash into the Twin Towers on the TV screen.

People started to come into the office for our scheduled issue briefing, but it was obvious that we should probably just go home. Those who came from Baltimore headed back out, and I headed home to find that my sister Janet was already there from her home. It took more than an hour to drive the five miles as the traffic was jammed with everyone trying to leave the Capitol Hill area at once.

Anyone trying to call almost any Washington, DC, 202 area code number on that day got a busy signal. The lines were jammed. I was surprised when my phone rang. It was from one of our Louisville news reporters wanting me to tell her what was going on. I really did not want to give an interview at that time. Like everyone else, I was trying to figure out where family members were—grandchildren, siblings. Your mother's call got through. She or your father Peter would be able to pick you both up from school.

The morning before, on September 10, I had just returned from Cape Town, South Africa, after attending the United Nations World Conference against Racism held in Durban. I flew into LaGuardia Airport. Had I been scheduled to fly back on 9/11, I might have been grounded somewhere in the world as all planes were instructed to land wherever they were and to stay there until further notice.

It took many days for air traffic to get back to normal. These were not easy days to say, *"Return no one evil for evil."* I had to remind myself that the Presbyterian Church supports the doctrine of "just war." Meaning, that there may be times when war is justified, but that we are expected to use proportional force when resorting to war.

One of the heartbreaking ironies of all this is that there was one of those little message notes on my desk saying that I was to return a call to then Secretary of Defense under President George W. Bush, Donald Rumsfeld. The note indicated that he wanted to have conversation about the federal budget surplus and what did the Church think. At the time, Donald Rumsfeld was a member of Fourth Presbyterian Church in Chicago. That conversation never happened as the nation prepared for more defense spending in the wake of 9/11. It is also worth noting that this was the last time the nation was to speak of a federal budget surplus. It was spent quickly, but not on the poor.

The Presbyterian Church Leadership sent a consoling and pastoral letter to the membership which said in part, *"as we all face the fragility of our lives, and seek healing for our nation's grief, let us lift up the Church of Jesus Christ and the Gospel that it is our privilege to proclaim. There is no earthly power, be it the power of wealth, the power of the military, or the power of political will, that can save us and undergird us in the face of the events of this day. It is only in the power of the Triune God, made known in Jesus Christ our Savior, and revealed in the power of the Holy Spirit, that we can find hope for ourselves, our grieving nation, and our broken world."* This was signed by Rev. Jack Rogers, Moderator of the 213th General Assembly; Rev. Clifton Kirkpatrick, Stated Clerk of the General Assembly and Elder John Detterick, Executive Director, General Assembly Council of the Presbyterian Church (USA).

March 18, 2004: Marriage Equality
"Just what did Ivory say?"

"Judge not according to appearance, but judge righteous judgment."
—John 7:24

It is hard to say which of the controversial issues in my civil rights portfolio was more volatile when it came to the wider church. It is evident that we are often so quick to judge the other person if their lifestyle does not live up to our own standards.

Even though the PC (USA) had progressive social witness policy on the right of a woman to choose to have an abortion and the right for equality in marriage, the contrary volcanic eruption that happened when I wrote about those issues did not seem to bear witness to those General Assembly–approved policies.

Of course, no one expected 100 percentage acceptance of what the General Assembly might have approved over the years, but that did not stop some people from wanting to put up a road block to advocating in Congress and to the White House with those policies.

Advocates know that when you win something, there will always be those who will fight to push that win back. As they say, "*There is no rest for the weary.*"

Currently, a session in a local church can give approval to a same gender wedding on its premises. That was not the case, in 2004, when I participated in a press conference along with Presbyterian Senator Mark Dayton a democrat from Minnesota and Senator Lincoln Chaffee a Republican from Rhode Island.

The senators pulled this press conference together at the last minute and toward the end of the day, long after those at the Louisville General Assembly Presbyterian office had gone home for the day, and strangely enough, I did not have home numbers or cell numbers for them. This meant that I could not alert them that there was a press conference on this issue coming up and that I had been asked to speak.

As is usual on such occasions, I researched our General Assembly policy to see if there were words about the civil rights of marriage. I did find that the GA supported civil rights in marriage. This was stated within the context of the Loving v. Virginia case having to do with an interracial couple wanting to marry.

I found myself thinking as I read the policy was there a kind of invisible ink there that said, "*except for same-sex couples*" or could this apply to all marriages, even same gender ones when it came to government sanction.

An article by John H. Adams in *The Layman Online* was entitled "Just what did Elenora Giddings Ivory, *director of the denomination's Washington Office, say about the Presbyterian Church (USA)'s position on same-gender marriages?*"

> *In a March 3 speech notable for its conflict with the denomination's constitution, Ivory said General Assemblies "have affirmed the civil right of same sex-couples to civil marriage," The Layman Online said, quoting from the text of her comment, which were e-mailed to Washington Office subscribers.*

In that speech, she also said,

Notably, while the Presbyterian Church General Assemblies have affirmed the civil right of same-sex couples to civil marriage, it retains its religious practice and view that "'Marriage is a gift God has given to all humankind for the well-being of the entire human family . . .

For Christians, marriage is a covenant through which a man and a woman are called to live out together before God their lives of discipleship. In a service of Christian marriage a lifelong commitment is made by a woman and a man to each other, publicly witnessed and acknowledged by the community of faith. [Presbyterian Church (USA) Book of Order W-4.9001].'"

Ivory's speech apparently caused a ruckus in Louisville. Stated Clerk Clifton Kirkpatrick prepared a list of constitutional citations and General Assembly decisions to ensure Presbyterians that the PCUSA has not endorsed same-sex marriages. That was originally posted on the Office of the General Assembly Web site, which, for the uninitiated, is hidden beyond the layers of other Web pages. Later, making certain that the church's position is not misinterpreted because of Ivory's comments, the beginning of the story was moved to the center section of the home page . . .

In introducing the stated clerk's compilation of statements on marriage, the Presbyterian News Services made no effort to explain Ivory's omission. And there was no public reprimand of Ivory, whose job is to advocate only for issues on which the denomination has expressed a view—especially the constitution . . .

The PCUSA story simply said that the stated clerk's compilation "came in response to public debate of a proposed marriage amendment to the U.S. Constitution and to complaints about the accuracy of comments made during a press conference in the nation's capital last week by the Rev. Elenora Giddings Ivory, director of the Presbyterian Washington Office.

Subsequent policies have determined that pastors and sessions are now able to make the decisions for themselves regarding weddings between same gender couples. The *Washington Post* on October 26, 2017, gives these statistics: "*Nationally, 62 percent of Americans favor allowing gays and lesbians to marry legally while 32 percent still oppose same-sex marriage. Three-quarters of Country First Conservatives oppose gay marriage. But Core Conservatives are now closer to evenly divided—43 percent support and 49 percent oppose. On the other side, 57 percent of Market Skeptic Republicans and 54 percent of New Era Enterprisers want to let gays and lesbians to marry legally.*"

This battle over same-gender marriages was not limited to the Presbyterian Church. It has been a matter of debate throughout other denominational churches and is still prohibited in several. Major newspapers across the country sent news crews to the national meetings to cover the unfolding of the issue as the locally elected commissioners to the various meetings discussed it.

As an issue of Civil Rights, do we as a county want to impose the religious views of any one of us upon another person? At the heart of the right of who to marry or when to bear children are opposing theological beliefs. Which should prevail and when should we stick up for the rights of those who may not agree with our own doctrine and perceptions?

October 28, 2005: A Tribute to Rosa Parks in the Capitol Rotunda

"For you were called to freedom, brothers and sisters; only do not use your freedom as an opportunity

for self-indulgence, but through love become slaves to one another. For the whole law is summed up in a single commandment, "You shall love your neighbor as yourself." If, however, you bite and devour one another, take care that you are not consumed by one another."

—Galatians 5:13–15

Andrew and Simon, you were just ten years old when your parents and I took you to the Capitol Rotunda in Washington, DC, to see the casket of Rosa Parks lying in honor. After her October 24, 2005, passing at the age of ninety-two, her body was brought to Washington so that she could be honored in a stately fashion.

We stood on the lawn in a long-winding serpentine line. It was a warm October night, and you were both very patient as we talked to you about what you were going to see and why this woman was and still is very important to so many people all across the nation.

It took a little over an hour for us to reach the inside of the Capitol and to see the casket as we walked in line in the marked off circle around the casket. It was beautifully carved in what looked like a red oak wood.

I cannot remember which of you quietly whispered, "She looks so small." In that massive rotunda, I too thought the same thing. I said to you, *"Small people can do big things"*—like biblical Daniel in the lion's den.

I pray that you can recall that image and that it has not been lost in time. It can serve you well when you may feel small in the face of your adult challenges.

May 2007: National Council of Churches Delegation to Middle East

"Seek good and not evil, that you may live; and so the Lord, the God of hosts, will be with you, as you have said. Hate evil and love good and establish justice at the gate; it may be that the Lord, the God of hosts, will be gracious to the remnant of Joseph"
—Amos 5:14–15

Although I served as the vice president of the Prophetic Ministry Unit of the National Council of Churches of Christ (NCCC) and a member of the Council's General Board, I was not present when this governing body was challenged by some of the elected women when they were discussing the possibility of yet another trip to the Middle East and Jerusalem for the heads of denominations. The women drew attention to the fact that the NCCC had always sent delegations that were made up of primarily men-and white men at that.

Therefore, it was agreed to send the next NCCC delegation composed of those of us who were in positions of justice throughout the member Communions of the NCCC. That this delegation would be augmented by a few young women. Although this would be my first trip to the area, it would not be my last as I would soon head to Geneva to work at the World Council of Churches as the director of the unit called "Public Witness: Addressing Power, Affirming Peace."

Of course we visited the holy sites and walked through the Holy City, going to the Church of the Holy Sepulcher over the site where Jesus was thought to have died. We also walked through the

Palestinian area of Ramallah on the West Bank and passed through several Israeli checkpoints. We saw the wall that was sometimes just a line on the street that separated Arab and Jew. We visited and listened to women as well as church leaders.

What struck me most was to actually see the growth and development of the Jewish settlements within the Arab territory. I quietly stated that they reminded me of the US white gentrification into the urban black cities in our own country—sometimes being done with disregard for the long time inhabitants. I was hushed with the suggestion to not say anything about such a comparison. Of course, I know that analogies and such comparisons do not always hold up. So I dropped it but have not forgotten this image.

Our group of about twelve women stayed together most of the time as we visited places where local women were waiting to tell us what it is like to live under occupation or violence along the borders. There was a free afternoon, so about four or five of us walked not too far from where we were staying to do a little shopping at the street market, sightseeing and to get some fresh air. Our walk drew the attention of a few small preteen boys who proceeded to taunt us. Calling us racist names, pointing and mocking us, making monkey sounds. No adult stopped them along the way. We rushed back to our guesthouse.

I remembered that Israel is dealing with African immigrant issues just as the US is dealing with a Central American issue of those coming across the borders without approved immigration statues. We know the US Jewish population to be friendly and supportive of the plight of the African American population in the US, but this is not the case within the country. Of course there have been the stories of black Africans who try to settle there after fleeing violence in their home nations, but we do not often see that they are subjected to racism.

This trip ended with a trip to Jordan, where we met with the religious and government leaders. On our last night, we were privileged to be invited to the private home of one of the woman leaders. We boarded a small bus that evening. The streets were narrow, and although our bus was small, it could not make a turn around a corner because cars were parked on both sides of the narrow street. It looked as though we were stuck there without the ability to go forward or to turn back.

But suddenly and unexpectedly to me, we saw about a dozen men jump out of cars that were ahead of us and behind us. They just lifted a small car off the street and placed it on the sidewalk. Our bus made the turn and moved forward. The men went back to that car, picked it up again, and put it back where it was originally. When we got to our destination, these men stationed themselves at all sides of the house and stayed there for our farewell party.

We were driven back to our hotel without incident. It was then that I noticed that the men stayed with us in the hallway outside of our rooms. They slept there all night. Jordan obviously did not want anything to happen to a group of American women.

The next day, we were scheduled to depart to the Jerusalem airport. A large stone needed to be rolled back in front of our Christian guesthouse in order to permit our departure in the wee hours of the morning before the usual time for the gate to open. Would the Israeli guards open it for us? We did not know. To calm my nervousness, I took out a piece of paper and began to write a prayer I promised to give to an upcoming publication in recognition of the one hundredth anniversary of the "*Social Creed*" for labor rights in the US. Here is my prayer entitled "There Are Many, Many Women" written on May 22, 2007 while waiting to see if the Israeli guards would open the stone to let us leave for the airport. The stone looked to be about twelve feet high. I completed this on Air France flight no. 2221.

There are Many, Many, Women

Lord, we come before you once again to ask your blessings upon the many, many, women of this world who struggle to bring meaningful and fulfilling lives to their families—particularly the needs of the children they nurture.

There are many, many women who

> gather ill-fed children to their breast that are
> depleted of sustenance because they them-
> selves have not received sufficient nutrients in
> their meager diets; we beg your blessing upon
> them . . . .

There are many, many, women who

> carry their children to separation barriers, barbed-
> wire fences, and concrete walls in search of health
> care for their children, only to be turned away
> with no care given at all or delayed at best.

We beg your blessings upon them . . . .

There are many, many, women who

> will face their first Mothers' Day without a child,
> who has been lost to war in some far away nation
> that they themselves may never see. We beg your
> blessings upon them . . . .

There are many, many, women who

> will flee bands of raiders that seek to rape and
> humiliate them only to prove what they believe
> is their superiority over another family of your
> people. We beg your blessings upon them . . . .

There are many, many, women who

> alone piece together limited resources to educate
> their children so that the entire family may some-
> day have a life that is abundant with the neces-

sities of living fruitfully. We beg your blessings upon them . . . .

There are many, many, women who

suffer physical, mental, and emotional humiliation at the hands of those who originally vowed to honor, cherish, and love them in marriage vows both given and received. We beg your blessings upon them . . . .

There are many, many, women who

find that they have happily conceived a child when desired, yet others who unexpectedly conceive and must make decisions about an unintended pregnancy.

We beg your blessings upon them . . . .

Lord, again we pray for the many, many, women who are often the brunt of the ills of all societies—both rich and poor. Give these women the strength to preserver, the fortitude of steadfastness, and a wisdom of what could be a more sustaining life that is full with the security and acknowledgment your wisdom brings to help us all to find our way out of no way.

1989–2007: Religious Coalition for Abortion Rights

"No woman is required to build the world by destroying herself."
—Rabbi Sofer, nineteenth century

I thought she was going to throw oranges, potatoes, or something at me as she briefly yelled at me with words I did not really hear well enough to be able to understand. I think she was speaking Hebrew in response to the wording on the back of my T-shirt. The front of the T-shirt had the words from the nineteenth-century rabbi above. The back on the T-shirt had in English, Spanish, and Hebrew: *"Religious Coalition for Abortion Rights."* She did not like that T-shirt. I still have it.

I served on the Board of the Religious Coalition for Abortion Rights (RCAR) later called the Religious Coalition for Reproductive Choice (RCRC) as a representative of the Presbyterian Church (USA). RCRC has over forty religious groups and denominations on its board. Presbyterians, Methodist, and United Church of Christ denominations were instrumental in its founding. RCRCs describes itself this way:

> The Religious Coalition for Reproductive Choice (RCRC) is a broad-based, national, interfaith movement that brings the moral force of religion to protect and advance reproductive health, choice, rights and justice through education, prophetic witness, pastoral presence and advocacy.

Defending the right of a woman to have birth control and access to abortion services in the case of an unintended pregnancy is an area where Protestants and Jewish organizations have worked on closely together.

During meetings of the General Assembly, there were always inroads by those who wanted to change this as seen in Overtures to the Assembly. This was one of the issues I had to be prepared to speak about and advocate for when asked to do so by the policy review committee.

Through many General Assemblies, I sat and heard person after person after person, give reasons why the church should change this policy and to oppose abortion rights. The reproductive health policies did not say that everyone had to agree to it. It just said that each person should determine in consultation with her family, doctor, and religious leader, if ending an unintended pregnancy is right for her.

There were those who wanted to change the policy to say that life begins at the moment of conception and should not be ended in abortion. Over and over again, we had to remind people that not all religious traditions understand that life begins at the moment of conception. Some religious traditions believe life begins at the first movement of the fetus. Others believe that life begins as late as the time of birth.

And should the life of the woman be taken as a first prominence, if a choice has to be made between her and her unborn fetus? Our PC (USA) policy would favor the need for an abortion in order to save a woman's life—as well as in the case of rape and incest. These were not easy discussions. I was among PC (USA) advocates who had to present this broad policy.

What I found disheartening in the debate process was that the majority of the speakers were usually men. These issues were questions about what was or would not happen to a woman's body, yet it was men who were the major speakers. They were adamant and passionate.

My perhaps extreme thought was that these men approached it as if it were an ultimate end action of a literal castration action on them. I never said that out loud.

At the April 25 March for Women's Lives, Rev. Elenora Giddings Ivory (left) welcomed church members from Washington State – Helen Bengtson Nash, Nancy Ellingham, and Mary Hanke. (Photo permission from American Progress.)

Our primary advocacy in Congress and within the church was for prevention of unintended pregnancy. In a June 30, 2004, story, the PC (USA) News Service reported my work on the *"Prevention First Bill"* that was in front of Congress at the time. The legislation was intended to reduce the number of abortions performed in the United States.

The bill proposed seven preventive measures: increasing funding for Title X, which provides services to women; expanding Medicaid family planning services; requiring private health plans to cover prescription contraceptives; providing $10 million for education about emergency contraception; requiring hospitals to provide emergency contraception on request to victims of rape; spending $100 million to support state sex-education programs that include information about both abstinence and contraception; and providing $20 million in annual funding of teen pregnancy prevention programs. When it comes to reproductive rights, we need to remain diligent.

Part 6

2007–2009: World Council of Churches of Christ Geneva, Switzerland

Presidency of George W. Bush and Barack Obama

I feel that it was an incredible honor to have worked at the WCCC. On my bucket list was always the desire to work in a different part of the world. The WCCC gave me that opportunity as I became the director of the unit called "Public Witness: Addressing Power, Affirming Peace." The position had many interesting travel situations. I filled my new and nearly empty passport in just two years there and had to get additional pages so that I could return home at the end of my work time there.

This honor came with a challenge to me personally as I had to constantly remember etiquette and protocols that come with international interaction when I was out and about and when religious leaders came to the building or attended the WCCC Central Committee.

Chief among these protocols was that within some religions, men and women do not touch as they greet one another. Without even thinking about it, we westerners just hold out our hand to shake that of the person we are meeting and greeting whether they are male or female.

On the other hand, there were other internationals who greeted you with a kiss on both cheeks. And then, I cannot remember if it was the left side of some orthodox leaders that I had to remember to sit at and not the right side.

I had to remember to keep my feet flat on the floor—do not cross your legs or even your feet. Once I put my mind to it, the protocol to not cross your legs or feet while sitting with some church dignitaries was not always hard to remember. But it was hard to remember to keep my hands at my sides. "Let all things be done decently and in order" (1 Corinthians 14:40).

I mention the leg crossing prohibition because it reminded me of an incident I experienced in my childhood. In the mid-1950s, I was in the waiting room of the family doctor with my mother, Phoebe Hill Giddings, and one of my younger siblings. As we noiselessly waited, a white woman got up and crossed the room to speak to my mother. She said quietly to my mother that she would feel more comfortable if she uncrossed her legs because black women were not permitted to cross their legs in front of white people where she came from. Without saying anything, I watched as my mother obliged her wishes and the woman went back to her seat across the room.

This waiting room incident took place before the passing of the 1960s Civil Rights Bill. Even though we were in the northern state of New Jersey, there were still times when you had to be careful of how and where you sat. My mother and I never talked about that incident, but I learned that there are times when you have do what you have to do in order to get what you want to get—like getting your child in to see a doctor.

I share this story about the doctor's office because there were times in the WCC position when I had to be aware of the protocols in order to achieve the primary given responsibility. For one, since women were not ordained in many of the communion member churches, I only wore a clergy collar just once and that was to preach on Sunday morning in a German Protestant church. It seemed to be accepted fact that although the Council someday might have a woman as its general secretary, she would likely be a lay woman and not a clergywoman.

So I tried to remind myself to keep my feet flat on the floor, hands at my side, and do not mistakenly sit on the inappropriate side of certain church officials unless invited to do so. A few key events for me, over my two years, were as follows.

January 30 to February 3, 2008: Kenyan Churches receive WCCC Solidarity "Living Letters" Visit

In the wake of the violence spurred as the results of the 2007 Kenyan Presidential Elections, the WCC formed yet another delegation headed by Dr. Clifton Kirkpatrick, who was the stated clerk and head of denomination for the Presbyterian Church (USA). Rather than just sending a formal paper letter during such times, the WCC sent a "Living Letter" delegation. More than seven hundred people were reported to have died in this violence and as many as 250,000 felt they had to flee from their homes.[19]

The Living Letters program sends fellow Christians to trouble spots as pastoral body representatives of the larger church. I was staff support to this delegation as was Dr. Aruna Gnanadason and Mr. Juan Michel. As with each of these visits, we met with church leaders, government officials, and social service individuals. We were hosted by the National Council of Churches of Kenya.

As had been the case in several African elections after the colonial power left the country, the first elected president had trouble stepping down when the time came as a result of a subsequent election. What is memorable from this trip was the time we were taken to an open field where we heard local people share their hopes and dreams for the future of their country. One gentleman stood up and recited parts of the US Declaration of Independence. As his supporting document toward free and clear elections, he recited these words that seem to have a deeper meaning in the middle of this field with the super-hot sun blazing down on us.

> *We hold these truths to be self-evident, that all men are created equal, that they are endowed by their Creator with certain unalienable Rights, that among these are Life, Liberty and the pursuit of Happiness.—That to secure these rights, Governments are instituted among Men, deriving their just powers from the consent of the gov-*

erned, —That whenever any Form of Government becomes destructive of these ends, it is the Right of the People to alter or to abolish it, and to institute new Government, laying its foundation on such principles and organizing its powers in such form, as to them shall seem most likely to affect their Safety and Happiness.

As I listened, I wondered how many people in the US really took to heart the words of the founding documents as this Kenyan did. In a January 3, 2008, statement the WCCC General secretary reported that *"Now is the time for leadership and statesmanship for the good of the nation from the leaders of Kenya's two main parties, the Party of National Unity and the Orange Democratic Movement. As leaders, they must turn urgently from partisan postures and negotiate in good faith to reach a non-violent political solution to Kenya's electoral dispute."* Other members of this delegation were the following:

- *Ms. Nyaradzai Gumbonzvanda*, general secretary of the World Young Women's Christian Association (World YWCA), United States.
- Prelate *Dr. Stephen Reimers*, member of the board of the Church Development Service EEDand representative of the Evangelical Church in Germany (EKD) and EKDs to the European Union, Germany.
- Ret. *Rev. Thomas Olmorijoi Laiser*, Bishop of Arusha, Evangelical Lutheran Church in Tanzania.
- Mr. *Graham Gerald McGeoch*, ministerial candidate of the Church of Scotland and member of the WCC central and executive committees, United Kingdom.
- Rev. *Stig Utnem* former general secretary of the Council of Ecumenical and International Relations of the Church of Norway.
- Dr. Geeske Zanen, World YWCA board member Netherlands.

Our trip was to take us to Nairobi, Kisumu, Eldoret, Nakuru, and Kakamega with changes to be considered based on ground conditions as local violence was still evident.

February 13–20, 2008:
WCCC Central Committee: Global
Warming and Climate Change

At this meeting of the main governing body of the WCCC, it had before it a proposed statement entitled *"Eco-Justice and Ecological Debt."* It was not well received by those world church bodies who had a problem excepting the premise that *"ecological debt, an increasingly recognized and researched concept and its reference to the debt owed by industrialized countries of the North to countries of the South on account of historical and current resource plundering, environmental degradation and the disproportionate appropriation of environmental space to dump greenhouse gases and toxic wastes."* This proposed policy wanted to say how the social aspects of indigenous peoples, particular in the global south, are impacted by the increased and over use of unsustainable ecological materials.

As the global north calls for more attention and participation in environmental sustainable projects, it appears to the global south that they are being asked to not advance in economic globalization by acquiring goods as they do in plentiful supply in the global north in order to save the planet. This is seen by the south as their being asked to refrain from advancement. The statement was hard hitting with sentences like *"the globalizing of economic models based on ever-expanding production to meet the insatiable consumption demands models based on ever-expanding production to meet the insatiable consumption demands of industrialized countries of the North has further undermined ecological sustainability. Climate change, the pollution of the atmosphere and water systems, deforestation, desertification, the extinction of plant and animal species and a host of other urgent environmental issues have disproportionately negative effects on impoverished nations, small island states, people of the south, especially women, farmers, fisher folk, indig-*

enous peoples who live in close relationships with nature, people with disabilities and future generations."

Although this paper did not go forward at that time. The WCC maintained a strong witness to the environment and ecology.

20

On a later 2008 trip to Fiji and the Pacific Islands, our group heard firsthand about the rising seas and how they are seen as threatening the existence of the islands and creating a new United Nation term of "environmental refugee." People are being displaced along the edges of our continents by rising waters due to climate change. The land is disappearing beneath their feet.

September 4, 2008: A High Level Delegation Was Asked to Visit Georgia and Russia[21]

I was standing at the kitchen sink of my Washington, DC, home when I saw the news report that hostilities had suddenly broken out between the countries of Russia and neighboring Georgia. I had been at home on vacation, and now it was time for me to return to Geneva the next day. As I listened to the story, I wondered if this would be something that I would have to deal with when I returned.

When I got to my Geneva office the next morning, there was a note on my desk asking that I immediately come to the office of Dr. Samuel Kobia who was the WCCC general secretary, as soon as I got in. The WCCC had received a request from the Patriarchate of the Orthodox Church of Russia—Alexis of Moscow, as well as from Patriarchate Elias II of the Georgia Orthodox Church to send a delegation from the WCCC to come help them find a way to bring their peoples together and to end the hostilities.

These Orthodox Church leaders did not see this as Russians and Georgians killing each other. They saw this warfare as Orthodox Christians killing other Orthodox Christians, and they wanted it to stop. We were to be seen as a humanitarian delegation and not to take side.

Although we had our suspicions at the time of our visit, it was not really known which side actually started the aggression. We had to go in as an even-handed delegation. We were to be a non-anxious presence in the midst of high tension.

I was to be the staff lead of the delegation. We were to leave out the next day as a delegation of five as follows:

- Metropolitan Nifon of Targoviste, Romanian Orthodox Church (church head of the delegation)

- Rev. Jean-Arnold de Clermont, Reformed Church of France, president of the Conference of European Churches
- Rev. László Lehel, director of Hungarian Interchurch Aid, on behalf of ACT International
- Rev. Elenora Giddings Ivory, director of Public Witness and Global Advocacy, World Council of Churches
- Mr Jonathan Frerichs, WCC programme executive (Middle East and nuclear disarmament)

A pastoral delegation from the World Council of Churches (WCC) will visit Russia and Georgia from 3 to 7 September. The delegation will listen to WCC member churches in both countries, encourage their efforts for peace and visit people displaced by the recent violence as well as church aid programmes.

"We expect this visit to encourage Christians in both countries to keep talking to each other and praying for each other," says Elenora Giddings Ivory, WCC director of Public Witness and Global Advocacy. "If Christians in Georgia and Russia manage not to allow the divide between their countries to separate them, they may help their governments to move towards a peaceful resolution of the conflict."

Arrangements for the visits were to be done equally in Georgia and Russia and had to be made as we traveled with our tickets waiting for us at the various airports as we moved from place to place.

The delegation expected to meet with high-level representatives of the Russian Orthodox Church, Georgian Orthodox Church, and others. The delegation visited humanitarian work of Action by Churches Together International (ACT) and its local partners. ACT International is a WCC-backed coordination body for emergency relief.

The itinerary was Tbilisi and Gori, Georgia, including the wartorn buffer zone of Gori. We had to fly to Riga, Latvia, and Moscow,

Russia. Vladikavkaz, is the capital city of the Republic of North Ossetia-Alania, Russia. Tskhinvali is the disputed capital of South Ossetia.

These were the bordering cities with residents of both wanting to split and be part of either Russia or Georgia. The headline of a September 9, 2008, WCC News article indicated that, *"After a 4,000 km detour, ecumenical delegation to reach South Ossetia." . . . a pastoral delegation sent by the WCC to Georgia and Russia has not been able to visit South Ossetia from the Georgia side of the ceasefire line. Un able to make the half-hour drive to Tskhinvali from within Georgia, they are now traveling thousands of kilometers to reach the enclave from the Russian side instead."*[22]

Since part of our objective was to establish humanitarian entree since the declared ceasefire, we wanted closer access to the midst of the destruction. We were told that there was one lone priest still at his church during the violence. The Russian soldiers told us that they did not want this international delegation going in as it might bring violence to us that would be blamed on Russia.

It almost felt like whiplash as we moved quickly in this five-day itinerary. I remember getting to Riga Airport in order to get to the Moscow airport and wanting a cup of coffee in the lounge. I had four kinds of money in my wallet but, none of them would be accepted to buy just a cup of coffee. I had Swiss Francs, British Pounds, US dollars, Kenyan money, but nothing would work—including credit cards.

The hostilities between the nations at their border did not come as a surprise to anyone who was watching the break down in the relations between the two nations. On August 12, the World Council of Churches and the Conference of European Churches called for prayers and assistance for those affected by the conflict in the European Caucasus, expressing alarm and distress at the use of force in the dispute over the bordering regions of South Ossetia and Abkhazia.

The local ecumenical organizations affirmed the interventions of the Russian Orthodox Church, the Georgian Orthodox Church, as well as the Evangelical Baptist Church of Georgia, all of which had called for a ceasefire, a negotiated solution to the conflict and urgent relief for those affected.

Our trip ended in Russia with a press conference arranged by the Rev. Vevolod Chaplin, who served as the deputy chairperson of external relations for the Moscow Patriarchate of the Russian Orthodox Church. He said to the cameras that "Only a madman today can declare all Georgians the enemy, and inflame anti-Georgian sentiment in the country." When asked, I repeated what I said days earlier to the Russian Foreign Minister when I was asked who we thought started these hostilities. Still not wanting to take sides, I used a mother's comment to her two children fighting in the back seat of the car while she is driving. *"I do not care who started it, just stop it and "in as much as it depends on you, return no one evil for evil."*

2008: They Forgot, They Forgot Executive Committee WCC: The Iron Curtain of Communism

"That same day Jesus went out of the house and sat by the lake. Such large crowds gathered around him that he got into a boat and sat in it, while all the people stood on the shore. Then he told them many things in parables, saying: "A farmer went out to sow his seed. As he was scattering the seed, some fell along the path, and the birds came and ate it up. Some fell on rocky places, where it did not have much soil. It sprang up quickly, because the soil was shallow. But when the sun came up, the plants were scorched, and they withered because they had no root. Other seed fell among thorns, which grew up and choked the plants. Still other seed fell on good soil, where it produced a crop—a hundred, sixty or thirty times what was sown. ⁹ Whoever has ears, let them hear."

—Matthew 13:1–9

*"The evil one comes and snatches away what is
sown in his heart."*
—Matthew 13:19

Lubeck, Germany

"They forgot, they forgot." This is a term that has stuck with me
since the first time I heard it on a trip to Lubeck, Germany, as a
WCCC staff person whose responsibilities included meeting with its
executive committee as the Public Witness and International Affairs
director. This committee met about every eighteen months in various
locations around the world. My Unit was responsible for the preparation of statements about the current world public policy—social
justice issues.

The executive committee did not want to go to Germany and
just sit all day in meetings, but they felt it necessary to have day visits with some of the churches in the region to learn more about the
type of ministries they were carrying out there. To that end, we were
divided into small teams and sent out to neighboring towns around
Lubeck.

My group of four had the furthest-away trip and had to pack an
overnight bag. We were sent more than an hour away to a place called
Rostock on the Baltic Sea in the northern part of Germany and east
of Lubeck. This part of Germany, called Rostock, was behind the
Iron Curtain during the cold war between western nations and the
former Soviet Union, in what was then called East Germany. We
were behind the former "iron curtain." Religion was forbidden in
East Germany for nearly forty-five years, by the Communist-run
government under Stalin.

While meeting with the newly emerged church leaders in
Rostock, we learned that even though the Wall of Separation
between those behind the iron curtain and the rest of the world had
been down for nearly eighteen years, they were and still are strug-
gling to re-establish religion in this former Communist-ruled part
of Germany where we were visiting. That is where I first heard the
phrase, *"They forgot, they forgot."*

The separation of Germany was over a forty-five-year period with people living in East German Communist isolation during that era. They had many cultural identifiers and practices taken away from them—including religion. Freedom of religion did not exist. Churches were turned into public buildings or housing complexes. When the wall came down those who wanted to reestablish religion and regular worship could not easily go back to the buildings that had been repurposed.

After the wall came down, people were free to practice religion and go back to church, synagogue, or temple, but not everyone could remember what that was like—hence the phrase "They forgot."

Imagine walking into a place of worship today and no one knowing what to do. You would know what to do. You know when to stand and when to sit, when to pray and when to sing. You know what to sing. They did not know this behind the iron curtain. They forgot how to do it.

Not only had they forgotten a lot, it had been so long that they forgot they forgot. Religion and religious practices were not part of their conscientiousness. There was no *nostalgia* for what used to be, because they just did not know it.

By the time the Wall between East and West Germany came down, religion and faith had been stamped out of the minds and hearts of most of two generations. For forty-five years, there were no symbols of religion like the cross, no religious stained-glass windows, no clergy robes, nor were there any religious holidays like Christmas, Easter, Hanukah, or Ramadan.

I actually like the fact that there were no TV commercials to remind you of how many days were left to do your Christmas shopping. There was nothing of the accouterments of religion that we take for granted in this country. There was no talking about God. So they forgot about God—they forgot about Jesus. Does that send chills up your spine? You did not pray; you did not say grace over meals.

The task of the Church, in the former East Germany and any of the few older people who might have remembered something, was to reestablish that memory that had been taken away. I wondered how many of the older folks with deep memories broke off bread to their children and whispered to themselves, saying the words of Jesus, *"This is my body, broken for you, do this remembering me."*

During the time of Communist control, they could not talk about religion openly for fear of punishment or even death. In some cases, two generations of people were born without a mention of religion. And therefore, many of them decided they did not need it after living without it for so long.

But God works in mysterious ways. In the parable, we heard that God plants little seeds that may sprout when and where it may not be expected. Once religion became known again in the general population, some of those new little seeds were in the young people—the teenagers and the twenty somethings.

As a way of being deviant against their parents, many young people started to join the newly reestablished churches in East Germany. The parents may have turned their backs, but the church was starting all over again with the teenagers in the communities. That's right; teenagers defied their parents by *going* to church. Young people were celebrating Christmas and Easter and they began to bring their parents to church. They learned again about the sacraments of Communion and Baptism. So many young baptisms took place. Perhaps this is like *"And the children shall lead them" (Isaiah 11:6).*

As well, I thought about my experience with these people of Rostock, Germany, when I read the parable of Jesus and the sowing of the seeds. Long before the iron curtain was in place, some of the people knew about religion and may even have been active in a church, but it was easy for them to forget it because the roots of their religion were not very deep. Europeans have never been great churchgoers anyway. Many of their churches are empty buildings all across many countries.

In some parts of Europe, the people did not know how to handle the religious buildings they had been given back. In the newly formed Czech Republic, some Christians were not quite sure they wanted the church buildings back because of the expense of upkeep.

With some people in Rostock, Germany, as in this parable from Jesus, faith was like the seeds planted on the rocks. When the negative forces came in, it was easy for religion to be stripped from their lives and from their memory. The roots of their religion may have been planted on already non-receptive hearts that were much like the non-receptive rocks in this parable. We must all ask ourselves, how deeply planted is our own faith and could it be easily forgotten in our own time or in one generation?

We know that some people quietly maintained their faith and kept it hidden. These were the ones who were like the part of the parable where the seeds were placed in good, deep, rich soil. And even though some may have had deeply planted and not forgotten religion, I can understand why particular ones may not have passed religion onto their children in order to keep them safe and the family safe who might say something religious in a hostile environment.

Verse 18 of this chapter of Matthew says that *"the evil one comes and snatches away what is sown in his heart."* So was the case of the evil sown by the oppressive government of the cold war Soviet Union era. It snatched away the faith of many. It snatched away Christmas—it snatched away Easter. There was no communion and no baptisms—because people were forced to forget.

So now, in Rostock, there are museums where you can go to see what a Christmas tree looks like and look at Easter eggs—view a

hymn book in a case and look at a timeline of religious history. I saw those paper garlands we made as children to put up as decorations. They were carefully placed in a glass case for visitors to see. The museum gave out small bags of candy that were called "LUTHERS BONBONs."

When we worship and say our prayers and sing our hymns and ask for forgiveness for our sins and bring praises to our Lord Jesus Christ—let us do so and remember—remember that this is truly a precious gift we have here. Let us pray that we honor that gift by growing our own faith and that of our children in solid fertile soil. For so many in this world, this is restricted and for others it is still forgotten.

Especially on Reformation Sunday, the day when those of us who are Lutheran or Presbyterian follow the theological tradition we called Reformed theology—meaning, that we are to be reformed in our faith and always reforming—God takes us on that journey. As in Germany and all around the world—God is reshaping and *reforming* us. Let us not forget it.

July 12–15, 2009: "Sexual Violence in Congo"

"Those organs of the body which seem to be more frail than others are indispensable, and those parts of the body which we regard as less honorable are treated with special honor. To our unseemly parts is given a more than ordinary seemliness, whereas our seemly parts need no adorning."
—1 Corinthians 12:22

This was a four-member delegation. I came away from this trip, thinking that the word "rape" is too mild a word to be used to describe what was happening along the eastern border of the Democratic Republic of Congo (DRC) that it shared with the neighboring country of Rwanda. What we found was the brutalization of women with regard to their bodies and their dignity.

As rape is generally understood, it is carried out in private and often leaves the women physically in tack. In the DRC border, communities of North and South Kivu as well as their surrounding villages of Goma and Bakuva, these attacks upon women were deliberately brutal. They took place at any time during the day or night in full view of neighbors, husbands, children, in-laws, and friends.

In 2009, the sexual brutalization of women had become almost a spectator sport on the part of the remaining post Rwanda genocide troops who still remained in the nearby forest. A woman as old as seventy or a girl as young as two could be sexually attacked by up to ten men.

A report of the humanitarian situation in the South Kivu Province stated that

> *in the South Kivu Province in the eastern part of the Democratic Republic of Congo there is a resurgence of cases of violence against the civilian population in recent weeks. With the preparation of military oper-ations to hunt down the FDLR fighters (Democratic Forces for the Liberation of Rwanda), Civilians are victims of theft, extortion, murder, home invasion and rape. Many abuses are perpetrated by men with weapons such as the Congolese Army (FARDC) and armed groups such as Mayi, etc. With such a secu-rity situation, civilians are moving in great number to seek refuge in areas which they think are more secured.*

When asked what the assailants hope to accomplish through such brutal attacks on the women of Congo, the response from some local pastors, the doctors at Panzi Hospital and the personnel at Centre d'Assistance Medico-Psychosociale (a trauma clinic) shared these thoughts with our group:

1) These are not for sexual gratification.
2) These are for the deliberate purpose of humiliation and to break the bonds of the family.
3) These attacks are to undermine the authority figure who is to be replaced by the brutalizer.
4) These attacks are designed to annihilate the next genera-tion of Congolese by preventing the ability to give birth in

the future or holding the woman captive until she becomes pregnant by her non-Congolese capture.

5) To deliberately transmit the HIV virus.

6) To establish rape and brutalization as an appropriate weapon of war.

Some readers of this essay may think that this is an act isolated to these hostilities between Rwanda and the DRC. But it is not. Rape is a product of war wherever and whenever it occurs in the world. It is not just the bonds of the family that is to be broken by such conduct; it is also the relationship to any authority figure. Men were also sexually brutalized. A local pastor was sodomized in full public view while his wife was raped. This destroyed the authority the couple had with the congregation and within the community.

Approximately 85 percent of the attacks are of the brutalized type, while 15 percent of women are taken as forced wives of the Democratic Forces for the Liberation of Rwanda (FDLR) soldiers. Another 5 percent of the rapes are of the usual type found in many parts of the world.

Dr. Mudwege Denis of the Panzi hospital,[23] asked that we get the word out about what was happening there in South Kivu, where they carry out the generally six-hour surgical procedures to repair the damage done to the women's sexual bodies with gun shots, knives, sticks, fire, etc. Panzi hospital saw its first case of brutalization in 1999 where the woman's genitals were completely destroyed.

During May and June 2009, there were more than 3,800 cases. The hospital has four surgery tables and a recovery room that will hold about thirty women for a twenty-one-day post-surgery stay. We saw this and learned that some women return to families who may stigmatize them further and not want their return while others simply stay on the hospital grounds after surgery with nowhere to go. They set up craft sales booths for any visitors to purchase the weaved baskets or trinkets.

While in South Kivu, we heard from several places that the rate of abortion has increased as women attempt to remove any evidence of the rape. Dr. Denis told of the Shabunda community's plan to kill eight hundred children who came from rape, but were stopped by the government when the plan became wider public knowledge.

Children who are born as a result of rape are often not acceptable to the families. The citizenship of these children is also questioned. Are they now Congolese as their mothers or Rwandan as their fathers? There had been thousands of these children born since the attacks began in 1994 with the Rwandan genocide. A look at the Wikipedia search for the hospital shows that it continues to be needed for this purpose.

Dr. Denis seemed unsettled with the question of how to get people to talk about the sexual brutalization when there is discomfort or embarrassment to describe what is happening while having to mention the parts of women's bodies that are not generally discussed in public. The WCC had trouble discussing this issue because it was said that the men in leadership found it difficult and embarrassing to speak of women's body parts. Dr. Denis responded to this with

> *The church must speak up and not remain silent as the world is silent. No one wants to hear about the way we treat the vagina. Even the woman will not speak of it. When they destroy the genitals even if we are ashamed to speak of it, the result is that they use our silence and fear as a strategy. We should not keep quiet. We need a campaign for women to break the silence. The silence feeds the situation.*

Many Congolese ask only for peace. The primary request from the Congolese people is the desire to have peace as indicated by the vice governor of the South Kivu region to the visitors of the World Council of Churches—Living Letters group. He asked specifically for a spiritual peace he thought the churches could help to facilitate.

A secondary need is for humanitarian support. It is true that the ongoing violence had created many internally displaced people (IDPs), but Congo feels that it can take care of its own needs if those attackers who are hiding in the nearby forest across the borders are removed. Many of the IDPs feel they could then return home. They do not need food, or blankets or tents as much as they need peace from the approximately seven thousand FDLR remaining military that need to be repatriated back to Rwanda.

> *"As of December 2008, it is estimated that nearly 250,000 people have fled their homes in the eastern part of the DRC escaping the fight that broke out between the army and rebels in August. These people have joined the 1,000,000 who fled in previous rebellions. The rebels say that they fight to protect the Congolese Tutsi community from being attacked by Rwandan Hutu rebels, who fled to DRC. Some of them fled after having perpetrated the 1994 Rwandan genocide. For a long time, the Congolese government seemed to have failed to stop the Hutu forces from using its territory. The situation would change due to the new development which has two important aspects: peace talks under the chair of the UN Secretary General's special envoy, General Olusegun Obasango, the former president of Nigeria. The second round of talks took place in Nairobi, Kenya in January 2009." (February 17–20, 2009, World Council of Churches Executive Committee)*

Among the WCC recommendations was that it must become known that at the root of the violence is the control of the mineral known as Colton. When each of us uses our mobile phone, we need to know that it is being powered by this mineral that is at the heart of the violence. Colton is a conflict mineral.

> *"The WCCC urged that the Rwandan government work toward the removal of remaining troops in the forest surrounding Kivu. That WCCC Member Churches, National Councils of Churches and Regional Ecumenical Organizations in Africa, encourage their countries to sign onto the United*

Nations Convention on the Elimination of all forms of Discrimination against Women (CEDAW), if they have not signed it or to implement it if they have signed it. And that member churches in other parts of the world do the same."

The world today presents complex power dynamics. Violence, social exclusion, political conflicts, competition for natural resources, and wars are the order of the day. Each of these issues cannot be analyzed or dealt with in isolation as they are interconnected realities. There is a relationship between political, military and social aspects that affects both the national and international contexts and has an impact on local communities. The WCC is uniquely placed to address these challenges, through its public voice and prophetic witness by addressing power and affirming peace, in response to urgent and emerging concerns of the churches in relationship to peace, security and justice. Such challenges and actions are an integral dimension of the work I was part of at the WCCCs and its mission as a global fellowship of churches.

Churches often call on the WCCC to accompany them in critical situations to defend human dignity, overcome impunity, achieve accountability, and build just and peaceful societies. The WCCC's approach addresses civil and political rights, economic, cultural and social rights and the right to development in an integrated way. The promotion and protection of human rights from an ethical and theological perspective includes a close accompaniment of the churches, sharing of lessons learned by churches, and regional ecumenical organizations. Continuing challenges included the need to further develop the inter-religious dimension of rights and dignity; the work on victims' rights, impunity, religious freedom and liberty and minority rights, as well as provide a space for the churches to discuss the relationship between justice, human rights and human dignity.

I wrote this poem as a preamble to the official report of this trip as part of the public issues document prepared for the WCCC Executive Committee in February 2009:

Congo is a woman—

A woman who has been raped by many nations for many generations.

The Portuguese first raped her in the early 1500s taking away as many as a half million of her children into the slavery to such countries as Iraq. And later the newly forming nation that came to be known as America.

The Belgium's raped her in the 1800's under the leadership of King Leopold II. *"By 1908 some 10 million Congolese had been murdered or died of disease and malnutrition- the worst genocide in the history of the world-half of Congo's population."*[24]

Congo is a woman—

A woman who has been raped of her riches for the benefit of the satisfaction of others.

Riches such as cobalt, copper, niobium—tantalum also known as Coltan used for our mobile phones.

Riches such as petroleum, industrial and gem diamonds gold, silver, zinc, manganese, tin and the uranium that can be used to make nuclear weapons to kill yet more people.

Riches such as coal, hydropower, ivory, and timber.

Most of all, Congo has been raped of her humanity. The world allowed her to be the subject of murder and pillage with impunity.

Congo is a woman—

A woman who has never been allowed to have her own identity. She has not been allowed to have her own dignity.

Her own leader Mobutu raped her in the late 1990's as he sold her riches to others and lined his own pockets at the expense of the needs of the people.

Her own neighbors of Uganda and Rwanda also raped her of her riches to sell across the nations of other continents.

Congo is a woman—

A woman whose daughters and girl children as young as age 1 have also been raped by those who were sent to let lose the ravages of HIVAids upon them.

Congo is a woman—

A woman who needs our prayers. A woman from whom other nations of this world must ask for forgiveness.

October 2009: Cuba:
My opening remarks to the meeting of Commission of the Churches on International Affairs:

"I am because we are."

The Commission of the Churches on International Affairs (CCIA) dates back to 1946 and serves as the original face of the

World Council of Churches of Christ to the government entities of the United Nations, World Trade Organization, World Bank, World Health Organization, and other public authorities. My role was as director of this entity. Its elected Moderator was Rev. Kjell Magne Bondevik who was the former prime minister of Norway.

We met in Cuba, at the suggestion of CCIA member Rev. Noel Fernandez and the invitation from Cuba Council of Churches, the Presbyterian-Reformed Church of Cuba and a *"I wish you a good meeting"* comment from Bishop Ricardo Pereira who was with the Methodist Church there. We were most thankful for your willingness to provide us this time together and to get to know you. Of course we are most thankful for the gracious hospitality of the Mantanus Seminary. They opened their arms to us made us feel most welcome. We worked very closely with Mrs. Moraima Gonzalez who at times must have wondered what she has gotten herself into. Thank you all.

We spent time with local projects and local churches. We encountered the people and the churches and listened to their needs and concerns. We have been richly rewarded by the experience and hope that it will continuously shape the way we approach issues regarding this part of the world.

As the CCIA, we are charged with holding up injustice and to bring the light to it so that the churches and the world may see and respond accordingly through a lens that is colored with compassion and focused on righteousness. Our task is to figure out how do we bring that compassion and righteousness out in a written report?

It is the tasks of the Commission of the Churches on International Affairs (CCIA) to

- give advice on public policy and advocacy;
- give advice on programmatic directions, including analysis of systemic issues that underlie injustice and social transformation;
- address particular programmatic and policy issues, with a special emphasis on the aim of promoting a peaceful and reconciling role of religion in conflicts and on the promo-

tion of inter-religious dialogue as a framework for community building, faith sharing, and understanding.

As we delve into questions of the current world financial crises and how it is in particular impacting this part of the world, but other regions as well, it is our hope that our findings will enlighten our final report to the Central Committee on this primary main topic of this meeting.

With regard to the financial crises, I recently heard one of the economic prognosticators say that the financial crises will turn around more quickly for the US economy as it may be forced to bring outsourced businesses back to the US in order to salvage what is left of their businesses. If this is true, the rest of the world may see this as protectionism. If this is true, it will have a greater impact on the economies of the rest of the world where their economies were really just beginning to develop. What is our responsibility here as churches? What should be said about the global economy? Where is the morality here?

In recent times, I have given thought to the African phrase, "*I am because we are.*" *I* am because *we* are. Perhaps we should look at the crises through that lens "I am because we are." Westerners are often accused of promoting to "I" over against and at the expense of the "we." That rugged individualism you see portrayed in old American movies about the settlement of the western part of the country, with actors like John Wayne who conquered everything in sight. I always felt so sorry for the horse he rode off on into the sunset, because it seemed so small for his big body. That is probably the image other parts of the world see when they think of the US.

On the other hand, Southern hemisphere cultures are accused by westerners of promoting the "we" at the expense of the needs and rights of the "I" individual.

Even our various church polities are also at various points on the spectrum between the "I" and the "we." Some of us are in churches where the views of the individual are taken into consideration as we use a congregational approach to our decision-making. Others of us are to wait as a group of adherents for directives from a person in charge of decision-making.

As a staff person for many years in several ecumenical organizations, I have sat in the back or off to the side and watched as votes on issues and budgets and structures were taken. To pass the time, I would try to guess how a particular person would vote on an issue based on their church polity. If they came from a church that let individuals decide, they would favor that approach even in public policies. If they came from a church that had governing authority in a smaller body or in one person, then they would favor government policies that reflected that view. This is understandable.

What does this have to do with our topic or our ongoing work? Well, as we look at polices of government on the economy at this meeting, or policies of human rights, interreligious cooperation, we may have to ascertain if we are promoting the benefits that may favor the "I" or those that favor the "we." What approach will we bring to bear as we speak—of the "I" or of the "we"?

As I understand it, the phrase "I am because we are" is African spirituality and is the English translation of the word "Ubuntu" (pronounced Ooh-BOON-too). It means we are all connected. We cannot be ourselves without community. Our health, wellbeing, and even our faith should connect us to one another. The wellbeing of the "I" is caught up into the wellbeing of the "we," which is the community.

Of course we find this concept in our Christian faith as well. The apostle Paul illustrates this truth by describing the church as the body of Christ:

> *Now the body is not made up of one part but of many. If the foot should say, "Because I am not a hand, I do not belong to the body," it would not for that reason cease to be part of the body. And if the ear should say, "Because I am not an eye, I do not belong to the body," it would not for that reason cease to be part of the body. If the whole body were an eye, where would the sense of hearing be? If the*

whole body were an ear, where would the sense of smell be? But in fact God has arranged the parts in the body, every one of them, just as he wanted them to be. If they were all one part, where would the body be? As it is, there are many parts, but one body.

The eye cannot say to the hand, "I don't need you!" And the head cannot say to the feet, "I don't need you!" On the contrary, those parts of the body that seem to be weaker are indispensable, and the parts that we think are less honorable we treat with special honor. And the parts that are unpresentable are treated with special modesty, while our presentable parts need no special treatment. But God has combined the members of the body and has given greater honor to the parts that lacked it, so that there should be no division in the body, but that its parts should have equal concern for each other. If one part suffers, every part suffers with it; if one part is honored, every part rejoices with it." (1 Corinthians 12:14–26)

I would like to spend just a little bit of time pointing out a few challenges to our work at the ecumenical center but also to all of us as people of faith and particularly those people of faith, who are charged as we are, to promote justice. It will mean that I will stray a bit from the primary topic of financial crises to make my point.

As we are dealing with the needs of people, we often find ourselves also having to think about the rights of people in order to see a way for them to lift themselves out of poverty. Poverty and justice cannot each be approached in isolation of one another. Approaching poverty without justice can sometimes be just charity and charity alone may not bring the systemic change needed to bring about justice.

We see these themes of the "I" and the "we" of the charity versus justice, sometimes coming into juxtaposition as we go about the implementation of the mandates of our work. As an example, I would like to read something to you that I wrote as I was working on the Congo statement. The statement was approved during the February meeting of the Executive Committee. As you listen, ask yourself, where is the "I" here and where is the "we," or to use the Corinthians reading, which of God's body parts are considered by some to be "unpresentable." My colleagues Guillermo and Christina may approach me for using these terms in this way, but I will explain.

Taking poetic license, one of the private poems I wrote while working on the formal statement on Congo was this:

- Does the World have a ***Responsibility to Protect Women***
  - from being child brides,
  - from becoming instruments of war through the use of rape,
  - from being trafficked and sold as sex slave.
- Does the World have a ***Responsibility to Protect Women***
  - from sexual mutilation known as female circumcision,
  - from the denial of education in places that do not educate girls,
  - from unsafe factory working conditions,
- Does the World have a ***Responsibility to Protect Women***
  - from forced pregnancy or forced abortion,
  - from the indignity of "honor crime" disfiguring punishment,
  - from family violence.
- Does the World have a ***Responsibility to Protect Women?***

What is perhaps problematic with what I just read is not the list of violations that women in various parts of the world face every day; it is in how we name them or categorize them. It is in whether we put first the "I" or the "we"—the woman being the "I" and her family or community being the "we." How do we respect both, when there is this suffering and humiliation?

Even though there are some in the world who would not call these actions atrocities, world governments have given us a few terms by which to judge what I would call "atrocities." Terms like "genocide," "crimes against humanity," and the "responsibility to protect."

Let's look at each of the three terms over against my list of atrocities and can we come to the defense of women in these situations or any other violation of humanity.

2007–2009

Jerusalem and Palestine were among the areas of my work as the director of this Unit of Ministry with the WCCC. The Ecumenical Accompaniment Program in Palestine and Israel (EAPPI) was the chief focus of the work. On the website it says, *"The EAPPI sends around 100 'ecumenical accompaniers' (EAs) from different countries to vulnerable communities in Palestine, where their task is to protect and show solidarity with those communities, and advocate on their behalf. EAs also accompany the Israeli peace movement in their activities."*

Being in Israel was always a challenge as you had to go through lots of security gates to get from one place to the other, while not always knowing when you might cross the border from one place to the other into hostility.

Our group took a break from discussions and we spent a day picking olives while in Jerusalem. Olive groves were how many made their living to support their families or the work of their organization.

It was hard being there and seeing what appeared to be reminiscent of urban removal with the Palestine's homes being destroyed in favor of the spreading new Jewish settlements. I did not voice this out loud because this comparison was not welcomed by the locals. Even though empathy is to see and feel the pain of others, it does not always go over well when it might appear that we may be playing a one-up-men-ship with the pain of another. It does not mean that we see our own oppression as more abusive than the other persons.

As with all that appears in these essays, these comments are what my thoughts were as we toured the Israeli bulldozed destroyed areas of Palestine. If only we could learn from not just the history of others, but also from our own history.

Part 7

2011–2014: October 17, 2014: Garden Memorial Presbyterian Washington, DC, Moderator of Session

Presidents Barack Obama and Donald Trump

"If anyone will not welcome you or listen to your words, leave that home or town and shake the dust off your feet."

—Matthew 10:14

Andrew and Simon, I was asked to preach at the annual homecoming service for Garden Memorial Presbyterian Church in October 2014. Take these words to heart as they might give you support in your lives when it seems a bit daunting. There will be times when you will have to deal with situations that may seem to bog you down. As I experienced the situations expressed in these essays, I have had to move along after wiping the dust of others that seem to fall at my feet. Those are the people who may try to convince you that your dreams are not achievable and that your gifts are not worthy.

Scripture says to *"wipe the dust off your feet"*; today we might say "wipe the dust off your feet and keep on steppin'." Keep on steppin' to what is the right way to go in the name of Jesus.

It is hard to step when our shoes are heavily laden with the dust of the past. It occurs to me that each church we enter should have a mat outside for people to wipe their feet as they enter. They could wipe all the old dust of their lives off so that they could lighten their load and worries and would be open to new possibilities in their lives. They could become fresh in the Lord's blessings.

How often have you been in a heated or uncomfortable discussion with someone and you think it best to wait until the dust settles a bit before you come back together again or talk again. The dust may settle figuratively around your feet and onto your shoes, but it is still there. To make life smooth, we need to wipe it off and let it be.

Whatever a family member or friend might have said in a heated moment is still there. *You need to wipe it off—and let it be.*

Whatever some bully might have said to you in school is, still there long after you are no longer together in the same room-it is still there. *You need to wipe it off—and let it be.*

Whatever bad or hurtful comment a co-worker might have sent your way is still there even when you are at home. *You need to wipe it off—and let it be.*

Whatever hurtful thing you might even have heard at church, stays with you even through Sunday dinner, *you need to wipe it off—and let it be.*

The bad all lies like dust on our shoes and at our feet. Christ would tell us to *wipe off* that dust and keep on steppin' in his name just as he told the disciples to keep on steppin'. We have to climb our way to higher ground just as Old Testament Jacob climbed. Keep on climbing Jacob's Ladder.

Christ told the disciples that some people might not be quite ready to hear what they had to say, so just keep on movin' on for the time being. Wipe off that negative and let your shoes shine elsewhere.

We want to be in that place where we can shine. We want to be in that place where people can enter and learn how to shine despite whatever else is happening in their lives.

We want to be in a place where people can enter and take off that old dust that may weigh them down.

You may need to find new maps as I did when I had to find my way back to my old college and elementary school some years ago for a reunion.

So "wipe the dust off your feet," find ways to help others wipe off the dust from their lives. What are the maps that might help everyone to find their way to Christ through you and while you do that —keep on steppin'. Amen.

2014–2017: Southminster Presbyterian Church

Oxon Hill, Maryland—Supply Pastor

Gun control and the memorial to the lost.[25]

My last day with Southminster Presbyterian Church was April 30, 2017. It would be just over three years there when I depart as supply pastor. I called it my third retirement.

While with them, Southminster Presbyterian Church chose to participate in the *"Memorial to the Lost: T-Shirt Display"* as produced by Heading God's Call in recognition of all who died in the previous year because of guns in the Washington Metropolitan region. This display has given comfort to the families whose loved ones name appear on a T-shirt. The names often represent those who are from age one to eighty who died as a result of gun fire. I have felt blessed to have been with this group of Christ followers and feel that it is like the cherry on top of an ice cream Sunday that has been my varied career.

I celebrated forty years of ordained ministry with a service of song, prayer and word on September 4, 2016. Thank you to all who participated in this celebration. And again thank you to Southminster Presbyterian who hosted it. It was also good to have my family members present.

January 17, 2017

Moving Day

I have really enjoyed my ten-room Victorian home these last twen-ty-two years, but no longer want to be "fixed" to home repair, leaves in gutters, snow removal, etc. I plan to travel for extended vacations at least once each quarter while I can still do that. I am downsizing to half the space I currently occupy.

That means getting rid of "stuff." It was hard to do, but I did it. Although this is the only home they had ever known me to have lived in, grandsons, Andrew and Simon, understand why I want to go smaller. However, they did not want me to give away the red Radio Flyer wagon they used to pull in circles around my house for hours at a time. As college students, you have not used it or even thought about it in many years. It has been moved to your mother Cynthia's garage. I continued to use it for many years to do garden work. I will still have a garden at Riderwood off a Terrace, but will not need a wagon.

Part 8

Additional Service, Assignment, and Elections

April 23, 1980: The Executive Committee meeting of the *Council On Religion and Law*, unaimouly elected me to serve on their national board of diectors

April 12–13, 1983: Plenary speaker at the Forty-Seventh Annual Meeting of *ChurchWomen United* in New York State. Theme-Take Time. Meadow Hill Reformed Church, New Burgh, New York.

September 1985 to November 1989: National Capital Presbytery: Staffed task forces on Middle East, Central America, etc., Committee on Racially Inclusive Congregations., Black Presbyterian United, Women Clergy Group.

Circa 1986 to 1989: Served as chair of the *Committee on Social Witness Policy*.

October 14–16, 1983: Keynote address at "*The World Federation of Methodist Women,*" Notheast Region. Theme: New Dimensions in Christian Living. Casowasco Conference Center: Moravia, New York.

1985–1988: "The Nominating Committee of the Program Agency Board wishes to nominate you for membership on the *Advisory Committee on Ecumenical Relationships*, Class of 1985. You will act as the United Presbyterian representative from the National Council of Churches Governing Board." Signed Donald Black, Associate General Director (February 16, 1982).

January 29–February 1, 1998: *Presbyterian Health Education and Welfare (PHEWA)*. Plenary persentation entitled "In pursuit of happiness Psalms 127, 128, 144, 146; Proverbs 14:20–21; 16:19–20; Romans 14; James 5:11"

March 16, 1998: Princeton Theological Seminary, ministry class presentation entitled "*The Public Role Of the Church*"

July 14–16, 2004: National Black Religious Summit on Sexuality: Breaking the Silence. A Season for Purpose: A Time for Change at Howard Divinity School, Washington, DC. *"In Consultation with Her God: Affirming the Right to Choose"* (one thousand participants).

February 21, 2007: Panelist, Black History Month Forum, sponsored by the Cultural Proficiency Office, Black Congregational Enhancement, PC (USA) Louisville, KY. Theme: Two Hundred Years: *"Where Do We Go From Here."*

November 16 to 21, 2008: WCC's United Nations Advocacy Week, in New York. The advocacy week, organized by the United Nations liaison office of the WCCC in New York, brings together over 120 people working on advocacy issues in churches, national councils of churches, specialized agencies, regional ecumenical organizations, and regional advocacy networks. The group will focus on three advocacy areas: migration, climate change and Sri Lanka. The week will be marked by an overarching framework of *"Human Rights at 60 Years,"* as both the WCC and the Universal Declaration of Human Rights celebrate their 60th anniversary this year.

February 28, 2014: Invitation from Presbytery to serve on Committee on Ministry—three-year term.

September 18, 2015: Plenary Speaker: Synod of Mid-Atlantic-Women of Color, *"Women's Lives Matter"*

Part 9

Conclusion

"Non-White"

This concludes many of my adventures and encounters. A few last things to share here are what I call a few "pet-peeves" that you too may adopt as you hear people speak. For instance, I do not like the term "non-white" when referring to black or brown people. To say something is "non" in this way, is to compare it to something that is supposedly better.

I do not like the term "non-white." I am not non-white. I am black. I am not non-man. I am women. I am not non-short. I am tall. This is one of my pet peeves.

"Kum Bah Ya"

I also dislike referring to some not achievable or fanciful goal or intent as a "kum bah ya moment." Isn't this is a trivialization of a faith fulfillment moment? To ask God to "come by here" is not to be considered merely a whimsical unrealistic moment.

"Micro Aggression"

There must have been at least 250 flights to Louisville for me during my nearly nineteen years in the Washington Office. For these and other trips, I always had a suitcase partially packed and did my best not to have to check a bag. These were usually one overnight stay trips.

On one such trip, I left the office for an early evening flight in order to attend a morning meeting the next day. I often took a stack of newspapers with me as I used this time to catch up with my daily

Wall Street Journal, Washington Post, New York Times, and *Washington Times*.

On one such flight, I settled into my aisle seat and began to pull newspapers out of a carry on canvas bag that I had placed under the seat in front of me. As I went through the *Wall Street Journal*, a white man who looked to be about forty-plus peered over at me from his aisle seat and remarked that he did not know that black people read the *Wall Street Journal*.

I cannot remember exactly what I said, but probably something to the effect that there was no indication that the paper was only for white people. He did not say anything else to me after that and I continued to read my papers. Maybe, this was another stereotype broken here for him, but another racially insensitive remark for me to bear. This was one of those "micro-aggressive" moments.

Hopefully he went back to tell all his buddies, colleagues and family members what he learned, so that if they have an opportunity to hire a black person, they will know that some of us do read business periodicals.

Blessings!

Part 10

Endnotes

1. Howell Booster, Sept. 16, 1971.
2.

WAKE UP AMERICANS

Your Country is under attack by enemies, foreign and domestic, who are working to replace our time honored and proven values with . . . Unbelievable Degeneracy

The United Klans of America wants a return to the real America.

. . . When a girl was a girl, when a boy was a boy. When you didn't feel embarrassed to say that this is the best country in the world. When socialist was a dirty word. When taxes were only a nuisance, and the poor were too proud to take charity. When you weren't afraid to go out at night, when ghettos were neighborhoods. When you knew the law meant justice. And especially, when young men tried to join the army or the navy. When songs still had a tune. When criminals went to jail. When you bragged about your home state and your hometown. When politicians proclaimed their patriotism. When the clergy talked about religion, and when you took it for granted that the law would be enforced, and your safety protected. When the flag was a sacred symbol. When our government stood up for Americans, anywhere in the world. When most people knew the difference between right and wrong and a code of Christian ethics was not damned by the liberal establishment.

What happened, what went wrong, that is all you hear nowadays. Nothing really went wrong it's just that there were no watchmen on guard to be sure everything went right. Americans have become apathetic in the luxury and take for granted their paycheck and their new shiny cars and boats, and expect more and more. Americans don't really care if some foreign power is trying to take over, as long as their comfort is not upset.

When America was the land of the free and the home of the brave, apathy did not exist.

The UNITED KLANS of AMERICA needs the help of all White, Christian, Patriotic Americans in the fight against those who promote the demoralization of our youth with dope and smut; have removed God from our public schools; have promoted race mixing to pollute our white race, and openly praise and support the S.D.S. and Black Panther revolutionaries who are working to destroy our country to achieve their fanatical goal of WORLD COMMUNISM.

WAKE UP AMERICANS. Catholics and Protestants UNITE in the fight for the protection of your loved ones and our . . . . . COUNTRY. If the time reading this literature has taken you from your TV, beer or other good things in life . . . we're sorry. If conditions have become this bad in the past few years, imagine what it will be in the near future.

We are not alerting you because we have nothing else to do. Those that lack courage, best hide. Join with us today and fight.

United Klans of America
P.O. Box 103
Hightstown, N. J. 08520

United Klans of America
P.O. Box 2509
Trenton, N. J. 08609

FIGHT COMMUNISM

YOU ARE ELIGIBLE TO JOIN THE UNITED KLANS OF AMERICA, INC., KNIGHTS OF THE KU KLUX KLAN

—If you are a Native-born Loyal United States Citizen, 21 years old, a White Gentile Person of Temperate Habits, with Christian beliefs, and believe in White Supremacy and Americanism — Please Fill in Below.

Place an (X) at one of the following:
- [ ] I would like to join the United Klans of America.
- [ ] I am a former member of the Knights of the Ku Klux Klan and would like to be reinstated.
- [ ] I would like a personal contact.   [ ] I am interested in joining the Ladies Auxiliary
- [ ] Please send me more information.   [ ] I am interested in joining the Junior Order
- [ ] Enclosed is my donation of $ ....

My Name is _____ Age _____ Sex _____

My Address is _____

City _____ State _____ Phone _____

3.

INDELIBLE IMAGES

THE EVENT WAS THE CLIMAX "OF EVERYTHING BAD THAT CAN HAPPEN WHEN YOU LIVE IN A TOWN THAT IS SO HEATED UP," THE PHOTOGRAPHER SAYS.

STARS AND STRIFE

A CLASH OF CULTURES AT BOSTON CITY HALL IN 1976 SYMBOLIZED THE CITY'S
YEARS-LONG CONFRONTATION WITH THE BUSING OF SCHOOLCHILDREN **BY CELIA WREN**

THE INCIDENT on Boston's City Hall Plaza took no more than 15 seconds, Ted Landsmark recalls. He was set upon and punched; someone swung an American flag at him; his attackers fled; he glanced down at his suit. "I realized I was covered with blood, and at that moment I understood that something quite significant had happened."

What had happened was partly an accident of timing—a collision between a man walking to a meeting and young pro-

testers out to make a point, a skirmish in Boston's epic confrontation over court-ordered busing to desegregate the city's public schools. But in Stanley J. Forman's photograph, the symbolism of the moment—the anger, the flag, the staggered figure that happened to be Ted Landsmark—seemed to epitomize the frustrations and grievances of a city on the edge.

Boston's battle over busing dominated local civic life for more than a decade following a federal judge's 1974 order to

APRIL 2000 Smithsonian 21

4.   William A. Dunkerley, 1908. Dunkerley wrote these words for the Pageant of Darkness and Light at the London Missionary Society's exhibition The Orient in London, which ran from 1908 to 1914. Many hymnals credit the words to John Oxenham, Dunkerley's pseudonym.

St. Peter (Reinagle) Alexander R. Reinagle, 1836. Alternate tune:

- McKee, from an African-American spiritual, arranged by Harry T. Burleigh **(1866–1949)**

5.   http://www.brill.com/files/brill.nl/specific/downloads/31985_Brochure.pdf

6.   NCCC Statement: "The Gospel According to '60 Minutes'- Response to '60 Minutes 'segment on the church. January 23, 1983.

7.

The Unification Church
International Marriage
for
World Peace and Happiness
through Ideal Families

July 1, 1982

Madison Square Garden
New York City

The honor of your presence
is requested at
The Unification Church
International Marriage
for
World Peace and Happiness
through Ideal Families
Thursday, the first of July
nineteen hundred and eighty-two
at eleven o'clock
Madison Square Garden
New York City

A special entertainment program
will follow that evening

Please exchange this invitation for admission tickets
upon arrival in New York City
at the Felt Forum Box Office
Madison Square Garden
on 8th Avenue, between 31st & 33rd Streets
beginning June 29th between 10 a.m. - 7 p.m.

8.   Matilda R. Cuomo, taken by Michael E. AcL 1984.
9.   http://www.oikoumene.org/en/resources/documents/commissions/faith-and-order/i-unity-the-church-and-its-mission/baptism-eucharist-and-ministry-faith-and-order-paper-no-111-the-lima-text.
10. *All I Really Need To Know I Learned in Kindergarten*, Robert Fulghum. New York: Villard Books, 1988. 196 pages ISBN 978-0-394-57102-7.
11. Picture taken by Elenora Giddings Ivory. Oct. 1986. Salvador, Brazil, Convention Hotel. Left to right: Rev. Paul Fernandez Caliene, Denver, CO; Mr. Mario Dabala, Dep. Colonia, Uruguay; Rev. Elayne Amityia Hyman; Washington, DC; Rev. Jose Roberto Caralcante, Copacabana, Brazil; Rev. Jill Martinez, Stockton, CA; Rev. Odair Pedrose Mateus, San Palo,

Brazil; Rev Alvaro Vega, San Jose, Costa Rica; Rev. Mary Gene Boteler, Auburn, AL; Rev. Gary Miller, Connersville, IN.

12. Picture taken by Elenora Giddings Ivory. Oct. 1986.

13. With Kirkpatrick and Ivory gone, what is the future of the PCUSA?

The Layman October–November 2007 Volume 40, number 3, the Presbyterian Church (USA) stands at a crossroads:

Will the denomination's decades-long slide into theological pluralism continue its ongoing dilution of the Gospel in the world, the hemorrhaging of its members and churches, the reduction of its staff and missionary force, the annual cutting of its budget and services?

Or will it rise up and reclaim its historic place as a beacon of hope in a troubled world by proclaiming – without hesitation or excuses – that Jesus Christ alone is the way, the truth and the life and that the denomination operates solely within traditional, orthodox Christianity in the Reformed tradition? Will it abandon its political alliances and secular, political accommodation and return to a mission emphasis and an increased commitment to the Great Commission?

In the midst of this crossroads comes the announcement that two people who have been lightning rods for what ails the Presbyterian Church (USA) – Clifton Kirkpatrick and Elenora Giddings Ivory – are leaving their positions within the denomination:

• Kirkpatrick – who has been at the center of controversy as stated clerk over such issues as ordination standards; the report of the Theological Task Force on Peace, Unity and Purity; the preparation of "The Louisville Papers;" and others – has announced that he will not seek a fourth term in office and will retire when his current term expires at the 2008 General Assembly.

• Giddings Ivory sparked controversy by urging Congress in 2004 to reject a proposed Federal Marriage Amendment, and by criticizing a 2007 U.S. Supreme Court ruling that upheld a ban on partial-birth abortion. She said the ruling "basically determined that the law does not violate a woman's constitutional right to choose abortion." She also was identified in 2003 as a longtime director of an organization that formally is aligned with groups promoting atheism, humanism, secularism, skepticism and Wicca. She is leaving as the head of the denomination's lobbying office in Washington, D.C., after 18 years to become the director of the Public Witness: Addressing Power and Affirming Peace program with the World Council of Churches.

Some people believe their departures may signal a possible change for the better in the denomination. Others, like Gashland Presbyterian Church in Kansas City, Mo., say it is time to recognize that there are "some deep theological differences with many in the denomination and their tolerance of some very radical beliefs that . . . cannot be called Biblical or Christian" or First Presbyterian Church in Baton Rouge, which believes that "remaining in the Presbyterian Church (USA) and fighting for reform is not a viable option."

The tenures of Kirkpatrick and Giddings Ivory are symptomatic of the ongoing theological crisis that is fracturing the Presbyterian Church (USA). While we cannot forcast the future, we can rely on God's Word:

"And it shall come to pass, that whosoever shall call on the name of the Lord shall be delivered: for in Mount Zion and in Jerusalem shall be deliverance, as the Lord hath said, and in the remnant whom the Lord shall call." Joel 2:32

The Layman Editorial Board

14. https://clintonwhitehouse4.archives.gov/WH/EOP/First_Lady/html/generalspeeches/1995/plenary.html.

15. http://www.un.org/geninfo/bp/women.html.

16. More than twenty religious groups, including as principal contributors four national religious organizations,[1] created

and funded Inter faith Impact, a nonprofit corporation in Washington, D.C., "to advance the jointly shared religious purposes of its members, namely, to carry out their theological imperative to increase the possibilities for peace, economic and social justice." Interfaith Impact's charter states as its mission:

(1) promoting a public policy that reflects prophetic Jewish-Christian values, (2) advocating to the United States government the enactment of public policies that are just, promote peace and protect the environment (reflecting Jewish Christian values), (3) developing and nurturing people of faith. to be effective advocates for public policies that are just, promote peace and protect the environment, (4) maximizing the voice, visibility, and ability of member agencies and denominations or faith groups to advocate for[such policies], (5) educating. the general public on the public policy issues of major concern to the inter-religious community.

In the fall of 1991, Interfaith Impact "called" Bell, an ordained minister, to serve as its executive director. In the engagement letter, Interfaith Impact recognized that Bell's service would be an extension of his ministry with the United Church of Christ, in which he was an ordained minister. It stated:

We are happy that the four entities required by the United Church of Christ to recognize your ordained ministry in this position will do so. Those entities are you and your sense of call; the recognition of this being a place of ministry by your local church; the Potomac Association of the United Church of Christ; and Interfaith Impact for Justice and Peace.

The letter confirmed a financial arrangement that designated $25,000 of Bell's salary as "housing allowance" to enable him to claim a parsonage exemption from income taxes and a contribution that Inter faith Impact would make to the United Church of Christ's pension program so that Bell would continue to receive pension and health benefits from that church. The letter concluded, "We hope this will be a rewarding ministry for you."

Because of diminished support from constituent faith groups in the spring of 1995, the full explanation for which does not appear in the record, Interfaith Impact began to experience serious financial difficulties. In May 1995, the Presbyterian Church, one of Interfaith Impact's main financial contributors, decided that because of the financial crisis it would not allocate further funds for Interfaith Impact for the year 1996. It also conditioned fulfillment of its 1995 commitment on a complete reduction of force and vacation of the premises rented by Interfaith Impact. The Presbyterian Church explained, "The current situation is not to be seen as the fault of the current staff who are in many ways victims of the circumstances the faith groups find themselves in due to diminished resources."

In response to the Presbyterian Church's withdrawal of support, the board of directors of Interfaith Impact promptly effected a complete reduction of force, intending to continue the program's ministry with a volunteer staff. In its letter of termination to Bell, dated June 23, 1995, the board stated:

Your termination is based solely upon the financial condition of Interfaith IMPACT which has [led] the Board of Directors to enact a complete "reduction in force." In this termination, there is absolutely no reflection on the quality of your work.

The letter concluded, "I would again express to you my admiration and appreciation of your work, my regret for the situation that makes this reduction necessary, and my gratitude for the helpfulness which you are continuing to give to Interfaith IMPACT."

Several months later, Bell filed this action against the board of directors and against the four principal contributing religious organizations, challenging their expressed reason for ending the program and terminating his employment. He complained, in six counts, that the defendants (1) interfered with his contract, (2) intentionally inflicted on him emotional distress, (3) breached a covenant of good faith and fair dealing, (4) interfered with his prospective advantage, (5) wrongfully terminated him, and (6) that the religious organization defendants breached their pledge to contribute to Interfaith Impact on a yearly basis. The district court dismissed the complaint against the individual board members for lack of personal jurisdiction and against the religious organizations because of a lack of subject matter jurisdiction.[2] He appeals only on the ground that the district court erred in determining that it lacked subject matter jurisdiction.

II

In keeping with the First Amendment's proscription against the "establishment of religion" or prohibiting the "free exercise thereof," civil courts have long taken care not to intermeddle in internal ecclesiastical disputes. As early as Watson v. Jones, 80 U.S. (13 Wall.) 679, 20 L.Ed. 666 (1871) (decided on general common law and not constitutional law), the Supreme Court disavowed the ability to resolve a dispute between a national religious organization and one of its local churches based on differing interpretations of church law, reasoning that

All who unite themselves to. a [religious] body do so with an implied consent to [its] government, and are bound to submit to it. But it would be a vain consent and would lead to the total subversion of such religious bodies, if any one aggrieved by one of their decisions could appeal to the secular courts and have them reversed. It is of the essence of these religious unions, and of their right to establish tribunals for the decision of questions arising among themselves, that those decisions should be binding in all cases of ecclesiastical cognizance, subject only to such appeals as the organism itself provides for.

Id. 80 U.S. at 729. And later in Gonzalez v. Roman Catholic Archbishop, 280 U.S. 1, 50 S.Ct. 5, 74 L.Ed. 131 (1929), the Court similarly refused, on constitutional grounds, to force a Roman Catholic Archbishop to appoint the plaintiff to a chaplaincy which was denied to him based on an interpretation of Roman Catholic canon law. Justice Brandeis there formulated the rule that "[i]n the absence of fraud, collusion, or arbitrariness, the decisions of the proper church tribunals on matters purely ecclesiastical, although affecting civil rights, are accepted in litigation before the secular courts as conclusive, because the parties in interest made them so by contract or otherwise." Id. at 16, 50 S.Ct. at 7-8. These principles were applied more recently in Kedroff v. St. Nicholas Cathedral, 344 U.S. 94, 73 S.Ct. 143, 97 L.Ed. 120 (1952), where the Court refused, again on constitutional grounds, to intervene into a schism between the Russian Church in America and the Soviet-era Russian Orthodox Church over church lands, holding that churches must have the "power to decide for themselves, free from state interference, matters of church government as well as those of faith and doctrine." Id. at 116, 73 S.Ct. at 154.

Although Gonzalez and other cases allowed the possibility of "'marginal civil court review' under the narrow rubrics of 'fraud' or 'collusion' when church tribunals act in bad faith for secular purposes," the Court in Serbian Eastern Orthodox Diocese v. Milivojevich, 426 U.S. 696, 96 S.Ct. 2372, 49 L.Ed.2d 151 (1976), abandoned any "arbitrariness" exception, moving yet further from any role for civil courts in ecclesiastical disputes. Id. at 713, 96 S.Ct. at 2382. It has thus become established that the decisions of religious entities about the appointment and removal of ministers and persons in other positions of similar theological significance are beyond the ken of civil courts. Rather, such courts must defer to the decisions of religious organizations "on matters of discipline, faith, internal organization, or ecclesiastical rule, custom or law." Id. The Supreme Court explained, "[I]t is the essence of religious faith that ecclesiastical decisions are reached and are to be accepted as matters of faith whether or not rational or measurable by objective criteria." Id. at 714-15, 96 S.Ct. at 2383.

The question that we must resolve in the case before us, therefore, is whether the dispute between Bell and the four national churches is an ecclesiastical one about "discipline, faith, internal organization, or ecclesiastical rule, custom or law," id. at

713, 96 S.Ct. at 2382, or whether it is a case in which we should hold religious organizations liable in civil courts for "purely secular disputes between third parties and a particular defendant, albeit a religiously affiliated organization." General Council on Finance and Administration of the United Methodist Church v. California Superior Court, 439 U.S. 1369, 1373, 99 S.Ct. 35, 38, 58 L.Ed.2d 77 (1978) (Rehnquist, Circuit Justice). We conclude that the dispute in this case is ecclesiastical.

Bell's complaint against the four national churches centers on the Presbyterian Church's withholding of funding and its consultation with the other constituent churches in effecting a complete reduction of force of Interfaith Impact. Bell argues that the motives of these churches were not as benign as simply withdrawing financial support. He has alleged that board members were improperly focusing on taking over the Interfaith Impact ministry, or on his personal life, or on unjustified claims of financial misconduct. At bottom, however, Bell's challenge focuses on how the constituent churches spend their religious outreach funds. While it is possible that the Presbyterian Church may have harbored hostility against Bell personally, it is also possible that the church may have been acting in good faith to fulfill its discernment of the divine will for its ministry. Resolution of such an accusation would interpose the judiciary into the Presbyterian Church's decisions, as well as the decisions of the other constituent churches, relating to how and by whom they spread their message and specifically their decision to select their outreach ministry through the granting or withholding of funds.

Bell argues that he is not challenging the internal decisions of the national churches but their external conduct in interfering with his relationship with Interfaith Impact. He characterizes this as a secular dispute between the churches and a third party. This argument, however, overlooks Interfaith Impact's role as the joint ministry of its constituent churches and Bell's role as executive director of Interfaith Impact.

Interfaith Impact is not a secular organization with which the national constituent churches had a secular relationship.

On the contrary, Interfaith Impact constituted a ministry of those constituent churches, and this was understood by all persons involved. The national churches maintain that they were engaging in ministry as directed by scripture, relying on Deuteronomy 15:11; Proverbs 21:3; Isaiah 49:6, 58:10; Amos 5:22-24; and Matthew 5:14-16, which they read to describe spreading light in the world and pursuing social justice as core Judeo-Christian values. Their claim is borne out by the charter of Interfaith Impact which provides that it is organized "to advance the jointly shared religious purposes of its members, namely, to carry out their theological imperative to increase the possibilities for peace, economic and social justice." Interfaith Impact's religious purpose is also borne out by Interfaith Impact's engagement of Bell in its "ministry." Indeed, their engagement letter to Bell concluded, "We hope this will be a rewarding ministry for you." Finally, Bell himself treated his position as a ministry. He obtained approval from his church to engage as executive director of Interfaith Impact as part of his ministry, and he agreed to the designation of part of his salary as a parsonage allowance for tax purposes. In summary, in carrying out his duties, Bell worked to spread the shared religious beliefs of Interfaith Impact's constituent members and to promote their Judeo-Christian values.

As this court has previously noted, a person is a member of a religion's clergy "if the employee's primary duties consist of teaching, spreading the faith, church governance, supervision of a religious order, or supervision or participation in religious ritual and worship." Rayburn v. General Conference of Seventh-day Adventists, 772 F.2d 1164, 1169 (4th Cir.1985); see also Corporation of Presiding Bishop of the Church of Jesus Christ of Latter-day Saints v. Amos, 483 U.S. 327, 337, 107 S.Ct. 2862, 2869, 97 L.Ed.2d 273 (1987) (recognizing the importance to the religion's mission of activities run by closely-associated corporations); E.E.O.C. v. Catholic Univ., 83 F.3d 455, 461-63 (D.C.Cir.1996) (citing Rayburn in case applying "ministerial exception" to a professor of canon law); Scharon

v. St. Luke's Episcopal Presbyterian Hosp., 929 F.2d 360, 362-63 (8th Cir.1991) (finding a chaplain in a religiously-affiliated hospital to be a minister); E.E.O.C. v. Southwestern Baptist Theological Seminary, 651 F.2d 277, 283 (5th Cir. Unit A July 1981) (considering even non-ordained Baptist seminary faculty to be ministers for Title VII purposes). In light of this precedent, it follows that Bell too was serving in a religious ministry while acting as executive director of Interfaith Impact.

When the Presbyterian Church decided to withhold its funds from Interfaith Impact, causing the end of Bell's work at Interfaith Impact, the Presbyterian Church, as well as the other churches, made a decision on how it would expend funds raised by the church for religious purposes, which directly related to its outreach ministry and Bell's status as a minister. Such a decision about the nature, extent, administration, and termination of a religious ministry falls within the ecclesiastical sphere that the First Amendment protects from civil court intervention.

For the foregoing reasons, we affirm the judgment of the district court.

AFFIRMED.
FOOTNOTES

1. The four religious organizations, all named as defendants in this case, are the Presbyterian Church, U.S.A., the Board of Church and Society of the United Methodist Church, the Women's Division of the General Board of Global Ministries of the United Methodist Church, and the American Baptist Churches in the U.S.A.

2. Bell thereafter sued the individuals, as well as Interfaith Impact, in the District of Columbia, where the district court entered summary judgment against him. See Bell v. Ivory, 966 F.Supp. 23 (D.D.C.1997).

   Affirmed by published opinion. Judge NIEMEYER wrote the opinion, in which Judge K.K. HALL and Judge DUFFY joined. 777

17. HEARINGS BEFORE THE SUBCOMMITTEE ON THE CONSTITUTION OF THE COMMITTEE ON THE JUDICIARYHOUSE OF REPRESENTATIVES ONE HUNDRED FIFTH CONGRESS SECOND SESSION ON H.R. 4019

JUNE 16 AND JULY 14, 1998
Serial No. 134, Committee on the Judiciary
HENRY J. HYDE, Illinois, Chairman

Stern, Marc, Director, Legal Department, American Jewish Congress 54

❖ LETTERS, STATEMENTS, ETC., SUBMITTED FOR THE HEARING Berg, Thomas C., Professor, Cumberland Law School, Samford University: Prepared statement 23 Durham, W. Cole, Jr., Brigham Young University Law School: Prepared statement 133 Eisgruber, Christopher L., Professor, New York University School of Law: Prepared statement 34 Farris, Michael P., President, Home School Legal Defense Association: Prepared statement 172 Green, Steven K., Legal Director, Americans United for Separation of Church and State: Prepared statement 210

❖ Hamilton, Marci, Professor, Benjamin N. Cardozo School of Law, Yeshiva University: Prepared statement 41 Ivory, Reverend Elenora Giddings, Director, Washington Office, Presbyterian Church (USA): Prepared statement 204 Laycock, Douglas, Professor, Associate Dean for Research, University of Texas Law School: Prepared statement June 16, 1998 8 July 14, 1998 225 McFarland, Steven T., Director, Center for Law and Religious Freedom: Prepared statement 178 Nadler, Hon. Jerrold, a Representative in Congress from the State of New York: Prepared statement June 16, 1998 69 July 14, 1998 198 Nolan, Patrick, President, Justice Fellowship: Prepared statement 167 Raskin, Jamin, Professor, Washington College of Law, American University: Prepared statement 218 Schaerr, Gene, Attorney, Sidley & Austin, Washington, DC: Prepared state ment 50 Stern, Marc, Director, Legal Department, American Jewish Congress: Prepared statement

❖ PREPARED STATEMENT OF REVEREND ELENORA GIDDINGS IVORY, DIRECTOR, WASHINGTON OFFICE, PRESBYTERIAN CHURCH (USA) I am Rev. Elenora Giddings Ivory. I serve as the Director of the Washington Office of the Presbyterian Church (USA). Our Church has approximately 11,500 congregations all across the United States and Puerto Rico. I am here today to share with you our support for H.R. 4019, the "Religious Liberty Protection Act of 1998." We thought it would be valuable for you to hear the results of the data we collected in the annual session reports regarding land use difficulties and PC (USA) congregations. This data was collected during our regular annual statistical gathering process where we ask the sessions of congregations to tell us things like how many new members in the past year; how many baptisms and how many deaths. Question number 6, of the most recent survey asked, *"Since January 1, 1992, has your congregation needed any form or permit from a government authority that regulates the use of land? These authorities include zoning boards, planning commissions, landmark commissions, and (sometimes) city/county councils?"* Our Presbyterian Church (USA) forms are supposed to be filled out by all 11,500 of our congregations. The response rate for this last session survey was almost 90 percent of our churches. Rather than just sharing what is sometimes dispassionate statistical information of a survey, I thought I would share stories involving land use troubles experienced by congregations who responded to the survey. We wanted to know where there has been either latent or overt hostility to religious folks. Four of the stories came directly from responding congregations.

1. **STUART CIRCLE PARISH-RICHMOND, VA** The Stuart Circle Parish is a group of six churches of different denominations that have come together to provide a meal ministry. It also offers worship, hospitality, pastoral care, in addition to a healthful meal to the urban poor in Richmond. This ministry was motivated in direct response to the Biblical New Testament mandate of Matthew 25 where Jesus admonitions to feed the hungry and clothe the naked. Jesus said, "I was hungry and you gave me something to eat. . . .") This ministry operated for almost 15

years in one of the parishes. When it grew, as the numbers of the poor grew, it was decided to move the program to another of the member churches. It was at that time the Parish ran up against a City Zoning Administrator who interpreted the program to be in violation of the City's zoning ordinance which limits feeding and housing programs for homeless provided by churches to no more than 30 homeless individuals for up to seven days between the months of April and October. Since the hungry do not automatically stop being hungry between November and March, the Parish did not want to be limited in its Biblical Calling of ministry to the hungry. The zoning guidelines would force the Parish to move the program around to all its member churches and it would still be not be able to offer meals on anywhere near the number of days necessary. Moving the feeding program around would also keep the hungry guessing as to where to go for food on at any given time. This ordinance was aimed at religious organizations engaged in this clearly religious activity. The City's justification was limited to responding to complaints about the behavior of attenders (unruly behavior, public urination, and noise in the area), although the City was unable to establish where or when these acts had taken place. The Parish had to go to civil court to protect its first Amendment rights. Had it not been for the Religious Freedom Restoration Act which was in effect in 1996 when this case arose, the feeding program would have been shut down. This program was the fulfilment of a central tenet in the Parish's religious belief and practice. So many of our congregations that choose to stay in the cities do so in order to fulfil this central theological mandate of service. They do not want to abandon the poor nor do they want the political establishment to force them to abandon the poor. Stuart Circle Parish v. Board of Zoning Appeals of the City of Richmond, No. CIV. A.3:96CV930

2. **PALO CRISTI PRESBYTERIAN CHURCH; PARADISE VALLEY, ARIZONA**; 193 MEMBERS. Palo Christi was described as a church literally located in the middle of the desert. The church wanted to construct a "beach volleyball court" on one side of the church's property for the use of the church's youth groups. The only materials the church needed to construct the court were a volleyball net, sand, and railroad ties to surround the court and keep the sand in place. The proposed site of the court was near the church's property line with the adjoining property being the backyard of a residence. In Paradise Valley, churches must obtain a "special use permit" in order to use the church grounds for means beyond that which would ordinarily be expected of a church. Consequently, Palo Christi had to obtain a special use permit in order to erect its volleyball court. However, the resident whose backyard adjoined the church's property at the point closest to the proposed site of the volleyball court objected to the construction of the court. The resident was concerned that the noise coming from the volleyball court would keep him awake at night. In an attempt to appease its neighbor, the church promised to not light the volleyball court and also promised that no games would occur after nightfall. However, these concessions were not sufficient for the neighbor as he stated that he was often on call at night and thus slept during the day. When Palo Christi applied for the special use permit, the resident owner of the adjoining property voiced his objection. In Paradise Valley, residential desire, regardless of how minimal, takes precedent over the church's desired use of land even when the church is willing to make concessions. Thus, based on the objections of this one neighbor, Palo Christi's application for a special use permit was denied. At the present, the church still is without a volleyball court and one less ministry to the youth of that congregation and the surrounding community.

3. CHESTER PRESBYTERIAN CHURCH; CHESTER, VIRGINIA; 728 MEMBERS. Chester Presbyterian owns

a vacant, adjoining lot which faces on a street shared by fourteen residences. The vacant lot is under a covenant agreement stating that the lot cannot be used for anything other than a house without the approval of 50 percent of the other homeowners on the street. The purpose of the covenant agreement was to prevent a business from locating in an otherwise residential area. Several years ago, Chester Presbyterian needed to expand its parking lot and wanted to use the vacant lot as a part of its expansion. The church sought the approval of the homeowners to pave the lot, but less than 50 percent of the homeowners gave their approval. Despite the church's attempts to negotiate with the homeowners, the homeowners refused to relent. Chester Presbyterian did expand its parking lot to the extent that it could without infringing upon the vacant lot. Chester Presbyterian is presently extending its Fellowship Hall. The parking situation is as bad as it has ever been. Once again, the church contacted the homeowners about the possibility of expanding its parking lot into the vacant lot, but the majority of the homeowners again refused to give their approval. Chester Presbyterian went to court over the use of the lot and also pursued remedies with the city. However, all of the church's attempts were for naught. Presently, the lot still sits vacant, and the church's parking problems remain.

4. **BAY PRESBYTERIAN CHURCH; BAY VILLAGE, OHIO**; 2195 MEMBERS. Bay Presbyterian Church is a very large church both in terms of its membership and its church grounds. The church continues to grow and has occasionally acquired surrounding lands when necessary for the planning of future growth. Recently, Bay Presbyterian completed a 40,000 square foot, four million dollar expansion. Al though several homeowners in the surrounding community protested such an expansion, the city grudgingly allowed the expansion to occur.

A few years ago, the city debated whether or not to propose an amendment to the city's Constitution that would require a church, in addition to nursing homes and libraries, to have any proposed expansion approved by a city-wide referendum. The cost of the referendum would be borne by the group wishing to expand and would undoubtedly cost the group thousands of dollars before expansion could begin—assuming expansion was even approved. Although this debated amendment would have impacted all churches, nursing homes, and libraries, the amendment was primarily considered a way to alleviate the city's growing concern about the size and growth of Bay Presbyterian. While the amendment was never enacted or voted upon, the city is once again considering such an amendment in light of Bay Presbyterian's latest expansion and the church's growing need for another expansion project. Thus, Bay Presbyterian is deeply concerned about the impact such an amendment could have on its ability to minister to its members.

5.   FIRST PRESBYTERIAN CHURCH; BERKELEY, CALIFORNIA; 1455 MEMBERS. First Presbyterian Church is a relatively large church whose problem pertains to a church-owned building located on its grounds. The building was originally built in approximately 1923 to serve as a school. Over the years, the 9,400 square foot building served various purposes before ultimately being transformed into twelve individual apartments. In 1983, First Presbyterian elected to purchase the building since the church property surrounded the building on all sides. First Presbyterian continued to use the building as rental housing by making the apartments available to low-income families. However, due to the building's advanced age, its condition soon degenerated to the point that it was no longer suitable for occupation nor desirable for any other use. Consequently, First Presbyterian desired to have the building demolished. The City of Berkeley was upset

over the church's desire to have the building demolished because the city did not want to lose any rental housing. Although Berkeley pursued some possible avenues by which it could prevent the church from eliminating the apartments, the city could not find any possibilities that would work. Thus, First Presbyterian ended its use of the building as apartments and prepared to demolish it. However, while the City of Berkeley was unable to find a means by which to prevent the church from eliminating the apartments, it was able to prevent the church from having the building demolished by having the building landmarked based upon its construction circa 1923. Since the building has been landmarked, First Presbyterian is unable to demolish it even though the building is an "eyesore" in the middle of the church's property. As the building has continued to age, it is now completely unfit for any purpose. It has all windows and doors boarded shut. It would cost approximately one million dollars to return it to a useable condition and considerably more to return it to a desirable condition. The City of Berkeley has a 1994 law which states that the city cannot landmark a church building without the church's consent. The building on First Presbyterian's grounds was officially landmarked after 1994. The City has declared that its actual land marking was effective before 1994 and that the 1994 law, requiring the church's consent to be landmarked, cannot be applied retroactively. Thus, First Presbyterian is still unable to have the building demolished despite the current law which would support its position. First Presbyterian ultimately sued the City of Berkeley over this dilemma in California Superior Court and was victorious. However, the City appealed to the Appellate Court which overruled the trial court and found in favor of the City. Although First Presbyterian felt confident that they had strong grounds for appeal to the California Supreme Court, the ongoing expense of the legal battle was more than the church could bear. Therefore, the church did not appeal. After approximately three years of battle, First Presbyterian estimates its direct costs at approximately $170,000 with total costs somewhere between $750,000 and $1,000,000. Presently, First Presbyterian is still battling with the City of Berkeley, and the unused building remains standing on the church grounds.

IN CONCLUSION The legal cost of these challenges to congregations and ministries, robs a congregation of resources they might otherwise have used for the benefit of church or community programs. The $170,000 spent by First Presbyterian Church in Berkeley, could have covered the tuition, room, board and student fees for 26 African American students at Johnson C. Smith University, in Charlotte, N.C., The $170,000 could have paid for six or seven mission co-workers to go overseas were teaching or medical personnel are badly needed. It really hurts me to learn that mission money is going for legal fees and court battles. The Presbyterian Church (USA) is a well-established denomination with over 200 years in this country. We just had our 209th General Assembly meeting in Charlotte, North Carolina. That is why it surprises many people that even PC (USA) congregations would experience such difficulties. It is even more surprising given that we are perhaps "over represented" in local governments (like zoning boards and city councils) in comparison to our percentage in the general population. In addition, about 10 percent of the U.S. Congress is Presbyterian. I have often said the "P" in Presbyterian must stand for politics. That being the case, the fact that we are in so many places where decisions are made-we are still having trouble advancing our ministries. Even as an established Church, we have encountered regulations that would deny the fulfillment of our ministries. This gives further credence to the complexity of these concerns and demonstrates why we need passage of HR 4019.

We can only surmise what must be happening to smaller denominational churches and minority faiths. In a 1995 Presbyterian Panel Survey, another information gathering instrument of the Presbyterian Church (USA), we found that many Presbyterians are politically involved. The survey found that over 70 percent of Presbyterian members either strongly agree or agree that "it is important for Presbyterians to exercise their Christian witness in the public arena." The survey found that 64 percent of church members actively participate in election campaigns and 69 percent write letters to elected officials. This is a direct out growth of our understanding of the Gospel message, to be involved with community through our churches; through our businesses and through the political process in order to do what needs to be done during times of societal decision making and need. I want to thank you for this opportunity to share these concerns. We would be happy to provide additional information if needed. Mr. CANADY. Thank you, Reverend Ivory. Mr. Green.

18. https://en.wikipedia.org/wiki/Million_Mom_March.

19. World Council of Churches News, "Kenyan Churches to receive WCC Solidarity Visit" Jan 29, 2008 www.oikoumene.org/en/news/news-management/eng/abrowse/49/article/1634/keny.

20. Fiji welcoming ceremony-Elenora Giddings Ivory, Fernando Enis, Nansulrick Gerber. Fiji ceremony chief.

21. http://www.globalministries.org/news/mee/world-council-of-churches.html.

22. World Council of Churches News-http://www.oikoumene.org/en/news-management/eng/abrowse/35article/1634after- . . .

23. https://search.aol.com/aol/image?q=Panzi+hospital&s_it=img-ans&imgId=CFB7893C8D003C6742A2E5E737233D-66EBC82238&v_t=webmail-searchbox

24. "Africa's Broken Heart: The Land the World Forgot," Hugh McMullum, WCC Risk Book series, 2006. Page xiii

25. https://heedinggodscall.org/

About the Author

My lifelong work has been with ecumenical and interfaith advocacy through local, state, national, and international organizations with whom I have worked. This volume is about various aspects of that work. I am now designated as honorably retired by the Presbyterian Church (USA) after forty-plus years of ministry in both the pulpit and society. You could say that I was a religious action figure whose responsibility it was to establish "justice at the gate" where injustice exist (Amos 5). Proudly, I have completed this memoir in the form of essays about various actions and situations of my life. I have a BA from Douglass College-Rutgers University, NJ in political science and history and a master's of divinity from Harvard Divinity School in Cambridge, MA. I was once referred to as a lightning rod on the progressive side of public policy issues even though there was biblical and theological support for the stances taken.

CPSIA information can be obtained
at www.ICGtesting.com
Printed in the USA
BVHW03s0152280818
525256BV00005B/39/P